"CHAOTIC FREEDOM" IN CIVIL WAR LOUISIANA

"CHAOTIC FREEDOM" IN CIVIL WAR LOUISIANA

THE ORIGINS OF AN ICONIC IMAGE

Bruce Laurie

University of Massachusetts Press
AMHERST AND BOSTON

First published in paperback by
University of Massachusetts Press, 2021

Printed in the United States of America
ISBN 978-1-62534-632-2 (paper)
First published in 2016 by the *Massachusetts Review*

Designed by Sally Nichols
Set in Perpetua
Printed and bound by Books International, Inc.
Cover design by Sally Nichols
Cover photo: McPherson & Oliver (attributed),
The Scourged Back, 1863. International Center of Photography.

Library of Congress Cataloging-in-Publication Data

Names: Laurie, Bruce, author.
Title: "Chaotic freedom" in Civil War Louisiana : the origins of an iconic image / Bruce Laurie.
Description: Amherst : University of Massachusetts Press, [2021] | Includes bibliographical references.
Identifiers: LCCN 2021017178 | ISBN 9781625346322 (paperback)
Subjects: LCSH: Abolitionists—Massachusetts—Biography. | Soldiers—Massachusetts—Biography. | Fugitive slaves—United States—History—19th century. | Antislavery movements—United States—History—19th century. | African Americans—History—19th century. | Slavery—United States—History—19th century. | LCGFT: Biographies.
Classification: LCC E449 .L385 2021 | DDC 306.3/620973—dc23
LC record available at https://lccn.loc.gov/2021017178

British Library Cataloguing-in-Publication Data
A catalog record for this book is available from the British Library.

A NOTE ON THE COVER

The image on the cover of this book is the first of Peter, taken in late March or early April 1863. Inspired by Marshall S. Stearns and Henry S. Gere, this original image was the basis for what became the iconic portrait, likely taken at the end of April 1863. Both images are included in this volume.

For James and Becca

Contents

Preface

Unlike many who encountered the iconic image of Peter, "The Scourged Back," during the Civil War, I first happened upon the image in narrative. A few sentences began a quest to solve the mystery of how this photograph came to be. In 2014, I was completing a book of essays on five antislavery advocates entitled *Rebels in Paradise: Sketches of Northampton Abolitionists.* I struggled over a suitable strategy for shaping the conclusion. I was hesitant to follow the narrative into the Civil War and beyond because only one of the abolitionists in question, Henry S. Gere, took up arms against the Confederacy. Two of the others—Sylvester Judd Jr. and David Ruggles—had died before the war, and two more—John Payson Williston and Erastus Hopkins—lived until 1872 but had effectively departed the reform stage. There was not much to tell of them, but I assumed there was quite a bit more to Gere's story because of his wartime service.

He documented his nine-month hitch in the Union army in Baton Rouge, Louisiana, in a series of letters to his newspaper, the *Hampshire Gazette.* While I had not read through them, I supposed they told a story unto themselves, a story that could not easily be compressed and stuffed into my book's conclusion. In addition, I was eager to wrap up the book; so I took the easy the easy way out, writing that his stint in Union blue would have to "be left for another day."

That day came as a striking revelation. Gere's letters avoided the war tales that preoccupy most first-person accounts of the conflict chiefly because he was a noncombatant. He told of the humdrum routine of camp life, groused about the inequality in accommodations between the officer corps and enlisted men, and skewered officers he thought to be unfit for their rolls. No surprises there. Many wartime memoirs plowed similar turf. The surprise was his evocative coverage of his encounters with African Americans he'd engaged in Black churches and on the streets of Baton Rouge as well as at a local contraband camp—essentially a refuge for the enslaved in flight from bondage. An arresting passage came in a mid-April letter that rehearsed the circumstances that led to the making of the image of Peter. It read that a week earlier Gere had observed "one of the most horrid and singular objects I have ever beheld"—the "bare back of a negro" who'd been beaten by "an overseer." His friend and camp commander, "Lt. Stearns," was equally astonished, so much so that he "took him to an artist and had a picture made of his back."[1]

Gere's brief account of this incident was the first and most important clue that unlocked the mystery of the provenance of Peter's image. I had no idea what image Gere had in mind but knew that the next step was to identify Stearns. I returned to an account of their 52nd Regiment Massachusetts Volunteers in which I learned that Stearns was Marshall Spring Stearns from Northfield, Massachusetts. I then combed through the holdings of local historical societies and surveys of archival holdings to see if Stearns left any records. It turned out that his survivors left the paper trail of a family history in typescript and his correspondence spanning his Civil War service that somehow wound up at the State Library of Massachusetts at the State House in Boston. This came as encouraging news indeed, but I had read through enough diaries and epistolary materials to know that it can be terribly frustrating work, no more productive than mining slag heaps. I headed to the State Library with my hopes in check.

I was rewarded beyond expectation. Stearns's family history depicted a restless and aimless black sheep who had been knocked about in a marketplace that the rest of the family had deftly exploited. His father was a celebrated house carpenter who seeded mid-Connecticut River Valley towns with houses distinguished by fluted columns around entryways that sometimes stretched to side porches. The elder Stearns taught his sons his trade and brought them into his business, but for some reason Marshall held out. He lit out for California twice, once to try prospecting in the gold rush of 1849 and again to manage a farm in the mid-1870s, before returning home none the richer for it either time. I learned as much from the family history and scattered sources but next to nothing of his time in Union blue other than the fact that he was nearly forty when he joined up and entered the service as a lieutenant by virtue of having recruited a company for his regiment. I sat nervously at my desk in the library waiting for the staff to deliver a single box of correspondence. I was riveted from the start.

Stearns's letters to his wife, Sula, and mother revealed a rather ordinary man of light schooling whose unorthodox spelling and offbeat punctuation did not blunt his capacity for candid self-expression. He repeatedly professed his love for Sula and their newborn daughter in evocative language we rarely see from Yankees, least of all mid-Victorian Yankees, confessing at one point that he longed to kiss his wife's lips. He also charted his own moral growth and political development from a self-conscious Unionist to a matter-of-fact emancipationist—an abolitionist indifferent to the formal movement but very much an ally in spirit and action.

I only regret that I was unable to learn much about Gere's private life or marriage. Only a few years younger than Stearns, he left no correspondence, and his obituary was terribly anodyne on matters of the heart. All we know of his personality is that he had a gift for political ridicule and enjoyed telling jokes. A favorite gag told of a Yankee in Louisiana who said to his comrades that he'd just seen the rarest of all sights in the South—a schoolhouse. It spoke of a deep disdain for the Old South and its system of slave labor that Gere inherited from the newspaper proprietor who oversaw his printer's apprenticeship and informed the rest of his life.

The most relevant passages in Stearns's brief but revealing correspondence confirmed Gere's account of their encounter in early April 1863 with a man brutalized while enslaved and their decision to take him to a photographer. Which enslaved man did they have in mind? Dates on the verso side of the cartes de visite bearing image of "Peter" sent home by medics and military officers coincide with the photographic session mentioned by Gere and Stearns, convincing evidence that the enslaved man in question is who we've come to know variously as Peter, Gordon, "The Scourged Back," or "A Typical Negro," after a famous piece on him that appeared in *Harper's Weekly.* It's worth adding here that medics in Baton Rouge and elsewhere remarked that they'd encountered many enslaved people who were brutalized but took no action beyond dressing their wounds. Though more such images may well come to light as the field of photographic history matures, for the moment all we have is Peter. The fact that it remains the only such photograph of its kind magnifies the gesture of the two unheralded soldiers whose stories are told below.

Who took Peter's photograph? An otherwise discredited story about Peter in *Harper's Weekly* attributed the image to the studio of McPherson & Oliver. Two scholars recently cast doubt on that ascription, noting that the original image did not bear their studio mark and the studio itself was not known for portraiture. On the other hand, while the *Harper's* story was fanciful, it may have correctly identified the photographers. Theirs was one of only a few studios in Baton Rouge at the time and Mathew B. Brady, the famous New York (and Washington, DC) photographer who churned out copies of Peter's photograph, attributed the original one to McPherson & Oliver.

Moreover, though William D. McPherson and J. Oliver were not primarily portratists, their portfolio did include some portraits. The shadowy Oliver left the business within a year or two. McPherson was a New Hampshire–born photographer who followed the Union army into the South, landing in Baton Rouge before moving on to New Orleans, where he probably passed away in an 1867 yellow fever epidemic. There were at least three images taken of Peter, the two in early April and one or more at the end of the month.

The question then arises: who took the later images and why? It was natural to assume that it was McPherson, but I needed evidence, clues as to his possible interests and motivations. I once again returned to the archives, this time to the vast photographic holdings of the Louisiana State University Special Collections. I was surprised to see that the photographs he left behind did not include a single picture of Peter. (Neither did the thirty-three photographs that are in Gere's legacy at Historic Northampton.) Instead, there was a set of pictures of Confederate military installations, which confirmed hints that he was in the pay of the Union, as well as street scenes of Baton Rouge and pictures of the Union encampments on the fringe of the town. More interesting still, McPherson took pictures of plantations and enslaved men and women on their way to the fields and in the fields themselves. Such subjects were verboten for the moonlight and magnolia romantics of the Old South who often depicted white children on the laps of safe and caring Black nannies, the relatively privileged household staff far removed from the ruder regimes of the field hands. McPherson, by contrast, did not shy away from capturing the essence of Southern slavery. The photographer cum camp follower was a likely antislavery advocate whose images of Peter reflected his political commitments.

The experience of Gere and Stearns suggest a larger and more significant dimension of the Civil War. The men in uniform were not simply armed fighters, killers carrying out the orders of their generals and field officers, oblivious to their surroundings. They were also human beings with feelings, even if some were more malleable than others. Perhaps most were hard-bitten racists, if dutiful Unionists, who ended the war where they started, largely indifferent to what they saw of slavery firsthand or to the shifting, official objectives of the war. This group probably multiplied as the draft pressed greater numbers of young men into combat. For men like Gere and Stearns, however, the extra battlefield experience of viewing slavery up close and interacting with enslaved men and women was a transformative moment. It confirmed Gere's lifelong abolitionism and faith in the promise of emancipation, if not full racial equality. From his informal interviews of newly freed Black people, he took a much deeper appreciation of their quest for freedom and hope for a new and better future. Seeing slavery up close had an even deeper impact on Marshall Stearns, the humble Yankee villager who began the war as a Unionist but, moved by what he saw at his contraband camp, left as an antislavery advocate. What little we know of his life in the immediate aftermath of the war suggests that his transformation, if not formally political, was real and heartfelt. That it was incomplete and escaped facile categorization should neither surprise us nor diminish him. He was, like the rest of us, a person of his time.

I would like to thank the following scholars, libraries, and archivists for their assistance in helping me prepare this manuscript: Georgia Barnhill, Joshua Brown, John Higginson, Beth Carroll-Horrocks, Mary A. Crauderueff, Daniel Czitrom, Joel Fowler, Matthew Fox-Amato, Dylan Gaffney, Joanne Gardner, James Gehrt, Barbara Krauthamer, Larry Lowenthal, Silvia Majia, Cliff McCarthy, Marie Panick, Leonard L. Richards, Stan Sherer, Ann Shumard, Manisha Sinha, and David Silkenat.

I am especially indebted to Jim Hicks, executive editor of the *Massachusetts Review,* for his encouragement and support. Mary V. Dougherty, director of the University of Massachusetts, diligently oversaw the transformation of "Chaotic Freedom" from an electronic article into this book, with the assistance of the able and artful hand of copy editor Rachael DeShano.

As for me, it has been thirteen years since I retired from the University of Massachusetts, Amherst and fifty years since I entered this profession, a golden anniversary of a sort. I was lucky to have been hired in the heyday of the humanities and to have spent my career at the same institution. My retirement has been enriched by the persistence of friendships I forged years earlier with former colleagues who have since become lunch partners and drinking buddies—Frank Couvares, Leonard Richards, Roland Sarti, and Ronald Story—and three more recent friends, Dan Czitrom, John Sinton, and Philip Khoury. Jules Chametzky, who spanned those groups of friends, has meant more to me than I can easily express; it's enough to say that he's the complete comrade, enormously well read, caring, and lovable. Though I derive great pleasure from their companionship, I find myself increasingly appreciative of the special sustenance one derives from family. Our own family circle widened four years ago when our daughter Becca married James Herbert. They are now a loving and mutually supportive couple. There are few things more satisfying in life than seeing one's children form their own families, and so this book is dedicated to Becca and James.

"CHAOTIC FREEDOM" IN CIVIL WAR LOUISIANA

IN THE FALL OF 1862, when they both began a nine-month hitch with the 52nd Regiment Massachusetts Volunteers, Marshall S. Stearns (1824–1902) and Henry S. Gere (1828–1914) had never met. They shared much in common beyond their origins in western Massachusetts—"the country," in common Yankee parlance. They were the offspring of middling families who plied skilled trades through their long lives. Gere had been a printer and then a newspaper publisher; Stearns, a currier and later a carpenter. A decade and a half older than fellow troops, they were the father-like figures of the regiment to whom the youngsters looked for advice and support, though not on the field of battle. For not long after the 52nd landed in Baton Rouge in mid-December 1862, Stearns was made head of the contrabands (more formally Superintendent of Negro Labor) and Gere was made regimental postmaster. They were effectively noncombatants,

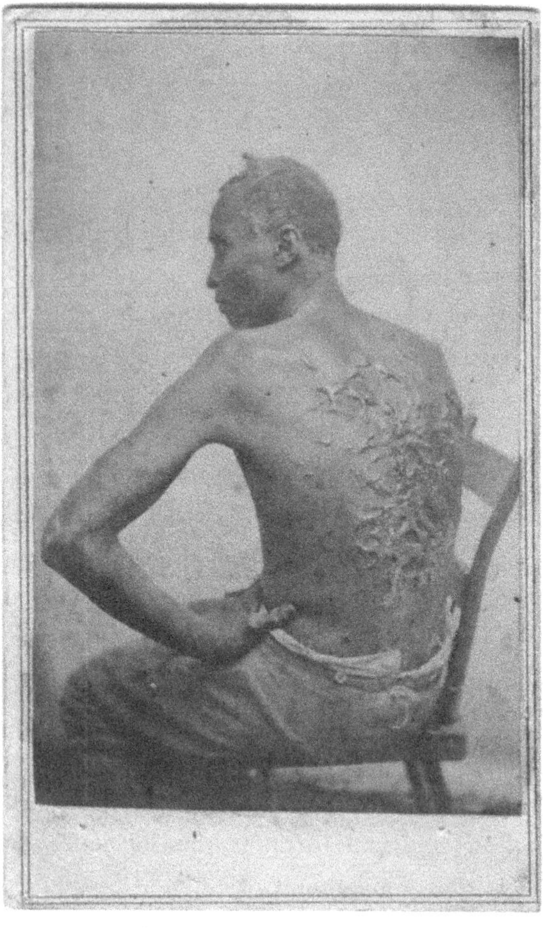

FIGURE 1. McPherson & Oliver, William D. McPherson, *The Scourged Back,* 1863. International Center of Photography, Purchase, with funds provided by the ICP Acquisitions Committee, 2003 (183.2003).

spared the worst of the war in one of its more disordered theaters. Yet they left us important perspectives, not so much on the blood-soaked battlefields as on the great social questions of race and slavery that were the cause of the conflict. The two men were also responsible for the production of the portrait of Peter, easily the most iconic image of an enslaved person that emerged from the war, his back a mass of sores and scars emblematic of the horrors of Southern slavery.

The motivations of the fighting men who served with Gere and Stearns have long engaged historians. At the risk of simplifying a voluminous and complicated body of historical inquiry, there have been two broad historiographical tendencies since World War II, depicting Billy Yank variously as a patriot or (broadly speaking) an abolitionist. Bell Irvin Wiley, the first professional scholar to turn his attention from the officer corps to the ordinary soldier, and longtime dean of the field, established Billy as a patriot first and foremost, a citizen who took up arms out of duty to his government. Scholars in Wiley's wake maintained that the terrors of the battlefield—buddies brought low by disease, mangled by bullets and canon balls, or killed and left rotting in the insufferable Southern heat—cured Billy of his idealism and left him something of a sobered pragmatist, preoccupied with his own survival and that of his embattled comrades. This school of thought downplayed the loftier matters of emancipation and egalitarianism, maintaining that Billy was apathetic in the face of slavery, even a racist. Wiley himself wrote that "a considerable number" of fighting men were "originally indifferent or favorable to slavery" and "accepted emancipation as a necessary war measure."[1]

The twin forces of the new social history and the civil rights movements, however, shifted attention from the perspective of the common soldier to the question of freedom. This school has tendencies of its own, but two stand out. One view is best reflected in the work of James M. McPherson, Wiley's successor as dean of the field. Though McPherson devoted his widely read and much admired *For Cause and Comrades* to refuting the claim that cause gave way to comrades, he devotes an important chapter to the question of abolitionism (if not race). Contrary to Wiley and others, he argues that between the summer of 1862 and the spring of 1863 the center of political opinion in the Union army changed, from indifference or revulsion to emancipation, to support for it.[2] The causal forces at work were twofold: the rise of Copperheadism at home and the performance of African American troops, first at Port Hudson, Louisiana, in late spring 1863, and later in Virginia and South Carolina.[3] A more recent, bolder work by Chandra Manning maintains that there was no transition to emancipation: both sides understood from the start that the "heart of the threat, and the reason war came, was either side's stance on slavery."[4]

This book offers additional insight into the motivations of comparatively ordinary soldiers—two men whose Civil War stories have never been told in full.[5] Henry S. Gere and Marshall S. Stearns brought different points of view to their wartime service. Gere was an abiding abolitionist, the kind of soldier described by Manning. Stearns had no obvious politics, and yet both men were strongly influenced not so much by Copperheadism or the heroism of Black men in uniform—though this bravery was influential—but by what they learned about race and slavery. They were appalled by what they understood to be the malice of bondage, yet also encouraged by what they learned from personal interaction with fugitives in greater Baton Rouge. Their role in the making of the image of Peter was no accident: it was a deliberate act that captured for them a powerful symbol of a system that could not stand.

In order to appreciate the historical context in which Gere and Stearns found themselves, it is necessary to understand the nature of slavery in Louisiana: the unique features of bondage in its heralded sugar parishes as well as the eccentric politics of the planters. At first the sugar barons were Unionists, and their treasonous politics made them fair game for vengeful secessionists, who fought a two-front battle against them and the Yankee invaders. The arrival of the Union army, as we shall see, sounded the death knell of slavery in parts of Louisiana, and its dirge was played by the untold thousands of enslaved people who bolted their plantations for the refuge of the Union lines, sometimes with the encouragement of Union officers. By December 1862, when Gere and Stearns landed in Baton Rouge to start their nine-month stint, the contraband camps and plantations run by Union officers bulged with Black men and women who had slipped the noose of slavery, typically in groups, usually at night, and always in joy. The two comrades were not passive observers of this extraordinary and unexpected social revolution, at once the dream of every abolitionist and the nightmare of every Southerner. Instead, each in his own way not only sought out runaways, but also befriended some. As a result, they acquired a deeper appreciation for the human cost of enslavement and a better understanding of its victims' aspirations for a future in freedom. Perhaps the greatest surprise awaited the end of the war, when Gere and Stearns—and other comrades of the Massachusetts 52nd—brought their convictions home.

LOUISIANA, THE SIXTH STATE to join the Confederacy, was one of the most diverse places in the nation, with a rich tapestry of ethnic and racial groups. There were French- and Spanish-speaking peoples of European origin whose ancestry dated back to the eighteenth century, when the region passed from Spanish to French control, as well as patois-speaking Acadians expelled from British Canada in 1754, the ancestors of today's Cajuns.[6] New Orleans was a magnet for English and Irish immigrants who did manual labor, both skilled and unskilled.[7] Its Black population differed as well. The vast majority of some 350,000 enslaved people were born in the state, but a good number originated in the Upper South and had arrived via the busy interregional slave trade based in New Orleans. A small but substantial number had been brought in from Haiti and, like the Cajuns, spoke a vernacular French. On top of that, Louisiana boasted the largest number of free people of color in the Lower South—some 18,000 out of 22,000.[8] They, too, were a varied lot of light-skinned mulattoes who worked as artisans as well as lawyers and other professionals. A select few were enslavers themselves.[9]

As for the economy, cotton was king but sugar was an able pretender. The value of the

Louisiana sugar crop soared to around $25 million at midcentury as the sweetener, once considered a luxury reserved for the best kitchens, trickled downward into the diet of ordinary people. It was grown in five zones, with a dominant corridor from New Orleans to Baton Rouge along the Mississippi River and the bayous, and several lesser patches—Bayou Lafourche and the Attakapas districts south of New Orleans; Pointe Coupee and Bayou Sara just north of Baton Rouge; and finally Rapides and Avoyelles Parishes northwest of the capital. The plantations of the sugar domain were some of the grandest in Dixie, averaging well over a hundred acres and each housing hundreds of enslaved men and women. In some sugar parishes Black people far outnumbered white: in Ascension Parish, southeast of New Orleans, the ratio was 2 to 1, and in French-speaking St. Mary's, on the Gulf Coast, it was 4 to 1.[10]

Historians have long abandoned the fiction of a feudal-like planter class, lounging on the front porch, bourbon in hand, averse to market capitalism and preoccupied not with accumulating capital but with preserving their honor.[11] Recent work discloses profit-minded entrepreneurs—some of the wealthiest Americans in the nation's wealthiest region.[12] Louisiana's sugar moguls were the first among these market-minded equals. They feverishly cleared and drained land, avidly purchased Black people in the New Orleans markets, and invested heavily in capital equipment, including steam-powered machinery that refined cane juice into granulated sugar. They consulted modern management manuals and kept meticulous records, determined to maximize efficiency and squeeze optimal output from their field hands. One popular manual advised against "excessive use of the whip," and the sugar men generally followed this suggestion, sparing the lash in favor of positive incentives. Enslaved laborers were paid for after-hours work, rewarded with their own garden plots, and given passes to visit kin and friends on nearby spreads.[13] Some former females in bondage interviewed by WPA agents in the 1930s recalled kind and considerate treatment. Ellen Betts, one of five hundred Black people on a plantation near St. Mary's Parish, said her master "am de greates man dat ever walk de dis earth." She was never "hit . . . a lick," and neither was anyone else, unless they deserved it. She continued that her master was an honorable man who never abused the womenfolk. "You couldn't find a yeller child on he place . . . sho' got no use for mixin's black and white."[14] Likewise, Aunt Virginia Bell, the enslaved house servant of an Opelousas lawyer, said that her master was a good man who "fed us good, too, and we had plenty of clothes."[15] Clara Brim, a field hand, declared, "Ole Massa, he didn't work us hard, no way," adding that he "let dem have de garden and dey can raise things to eat and sell. Sometimes dey have some pig[s] and chickens."[16]

But such memories amounted to one side of a more complicated—and darker—picture. Even the putatively kindest masters kept their chattel on a very short leash. Unlike Jamaican field hands with gardens, who peddled their goods in their own markets (and developed a sense of autonomy from it), their Louisiana counterparts had to sell their produce to their owners.[17] They worked such plots after hours in an industrial-like system that bore down harder and harder, not unlike the grind of the fledgling industrial mills of the North. These early-day factories-in-the-fields were supervised by unsentimental managers and worked by interdependent gangs of cultivators, cutters, and machine operators; their pace of toil stiffened in the harvest and the refining cycles from early to late fall. Planters and overseers meted out a range of punishment depending on the transgression. The enslaved person caught stealing from the storehouse or the master's garden could expect to be stripped of privileges or time off, placed in stocks or chains, or dressed in a "Louisiana shirt," a barrel with an open lid that was placed over the offender's head, locking their arms at their sides. They could not sit down or use "his arms . . . jus' walk roun' all day. . . ." The Louisiana shirt was an unpleasant, relatively mild form of shaming; the offender, said another enslaved person, had to bear the "brunt of other slaves' jokes."[18]

If the stocks and Louisiana shirts were designed to humiliate, the whip was designed to scar the offender, not only for the moment but for life. It was typically administered in graduated stripes, from ten up to hundreds, according to the personality of the master and the seriousness of the offense—so many stripes for slacking off, sassing an overseer, leaving without a pass, or the cardinal offense of running off. Abusive masters had a hair trigger, kinder masters a slow one, but none of them withheld the whip. Solomon Northup, the Northern-born African American who was kidnapped in Washington, DC, and taken to Louisiana, recalled beatings in vivid detail in his narrative *Twelve Years a Slave.* A friend and fellow bondsman apprehended while visiting a neighboring plantation without permission was beaten severely by his captors and bitten by their hounds. Not long afterward he was caught yet again for running off, jailed, and sent home to a brutal flogging, the "scars upon his back, which he will carry with him to his grave, perpetually remind him of the dangers of such insolence."[19]

The Federal Writers' Project interviewees who worked the cane and cotton fields may have had failing memories, but few ever forgot the sting of the lash or the bite of the hounds. William Matthews recalled that his master could "out-mean de debbil heslf," confirming Northup's account of the trials of captured runaways: "If dey run in de stream of water, de dogs gits after 'em and drowns 'em den Dick, de overseer, he whoop'em," and in a particularly brutal way—so particular, it seems, that Louisiana planters had whipping down to a ghoulish science of sorts. "He drive down four stakes for de feets and hands and tie 'em up. Den he whoop 'em from head to feets. De whip made out a hide, cut in strips, with holes punch in 'em. When dey hits de skin it makes blisters."[20] The blisters turned to scars and the scars into enduring reminders of what lay in store for habitual offenders. It was so common that Gere and Stearns could not fail to take note.

Enslaved women were vulnerable to unique abuse because of their gender and complete subservience. Masters in the sugar patches, writes the historian Richard Follett, promoted "slave breeding."[21] Masters encouraged their chattel to multiply for "de breedin," and it was not unusual for them to appoint particularly virile men, "studs," to father children. Willie Williams, in Vermilion Parish, told his WPA interviewers that his master, "anxious to raise good, big slaves" picked out the "big" males who "did no work but watch dem womens and he 'am de husban' for dem all. De marster . . . was a-raisin' some fine niggers dat way."[22] Nor were the more licentious masters above exploiting enslaved women for pleasure, a verboten topic in the big house but one well understood in their quarters. Julia Woodrich's mother was doubly a "good breeder" because she had fifteen children from different men and lived to see one of her daughters earn the same tragic reputation. "I 'member how my massa usete come an' get my sister . . . take her down in the quarter all night—den have de nerve to come 'roun de next day an' ax her how she feel."[23] Such coerced unions surely help account for the unusually large numbers of mulattoes and other peoples of mixed races in Louisiana, another vestige of its slavery that, as we shall see, left an indelible impression on Gere and Stearns.

The domain of the Louisiana planters was hurled into turmoil when the Civil War broke out. Louisiana eventually trooped out of the Union with the rest of the Lower South, but not without resistance from the sugar planters, joined perhaps by the more prominent cotton growers. The planters' close ties to Northern financiers, shippers, insurers, and marketers, coupled with their longtime dependence on tariff protection, made them reluctant to commit economic suicide in a quixotic act of secession. They were defeated in the critical election of 1860 and the secessionist convention in January 1861, but still polled well in both cases on the platform of Unionism. They remained Unionists through the early years of the war, persuaded that President Lincoln would countenance slavery if they brought their state back into the Union.[24] Their loyalty provoked a backlash from resentful poor whites in a reign of terror that burned Unionist buildings, trashed crops, and threatened lives, a civil war within the wider war.[25]

Secession also thrust Louisiana into the crosshairs of the North's military strategy. Lincoln and his generals planned to take control of the lower Mississippi River in order to open the artery to river craft and sever the region from the rest of the South. This tactic required sending Ulysses S. Grant's army south along the west bank of the river in Tennessee and Nathaniel P. Banks's forces north from New Orleans through Port Hudson, with both armies converging at Vicksburg. Banks's expedition to Port Hudson, scheduled to start in late spring 1862, was delayed until early summer. The first stage of the strategy, however, went as planned. As Grant moved into Tennessee, the Confederate high command diverted troops stationed at New Orleans northward, leaving Baton Rouge vulnerable to Northern gunboats on the Mississippi. A week of ferocious pounding from David Farragut's schooners softened Forts Jackson and St. Philip, on the seaward side of New Orleans, and on April 29 a contingent of marines landed. Two days later, on May 1, some 18,000 soldiers entered the city proper under Brigadier General Benjamin Butler.[26]

The state capital of Baton Rouge, eighty miles upriver, was a more stubborn target. In January of 1861 the secessionist government had seized the federal arsenal there in a farcical (though successful) occupation, but failed to hold it. A week after Farragut took New Orleans, Union soldiers took the capital without immediate resistance, but soon afterward faced occasional fire from Confederate irregulars. As Farragut's gunboats patrolled the river and land units dug in, the Confederates prepared to take back the capital under General John C. Breckenridge, the hard-line states' rights Democrat who had led the Lower South out of the Union and who would later become the Confederacy's secretary of war.

Breckenridge was also an able general of the seasoned troops, yet he would not be the victor on the morning of May 5. The fighting was short but furious and bloody, costing 308 Union casualties and some 450 Confederate casualties. The Union men spent a breakneck few weeks girding for a counterattack, mobilizing the fugitives who poured in from nearby plantations to build fortifications and raze buildings in order to clear the way to the rear of the town for the guns of the frigates in the harbor. The expected assault never came. The damage came instead from unruly soldiers, who ransacked homes and businesses, keeping what they wanted and trashing the rest.

Butler wavered on what to do with the ravaged capital. He first considered holding the town, then ordered it burned to the ground, before changing his mind again at the urging of an officer who convinced him that destroying an orphanage and other institutions would make him look unduly cruel. The reprieve saved Baton Rouge for Gere and Stearns, who wound up occupying the very institutions spared by Butler's change of heart.[27]

Butler can be credited with forcing a reluctant Congress and the president into the most significant policy decisions of the first half of the war—determining the status of self-liberated people in bondage. As is now well known, with the Union army's advance into the South, greater and greater numbers of enslaved people broke free and sought refuge within Union lines, first in Virginia, where Butler was in command of a force, and then throughout the Confederacy. Butler established the precedent of declaring such escapees "contraband of war," and instead of returning them to their masters, he put them to work as laborers for the Union army. Congress then formalized his policy by approving the first Confiscation Act in July 1861, which declared that masters whose chattel aided the Confederate war effort forfeited "all right" to them. As self-liberation spread during the rest of the year, Congress went a step further and passed the Second Confiscation Act, which declared the enslaved people of rebel owners "captives of war" and "forever free of servitude."[28] This measure set the stage for President Lincoln's Preliminary Emancipation Proclamation two months later, in September, which took effect the following January. The action left two problems unresolved in Louisiana: how to treat Unionist planters, whom the president desperately wanted to court, and what to do with runaways in southern Louisiana, since the region had fallen under Union control and thus was now exempt from the Emancipation Proclamation.

Butler in New Orleans, together with officials in Washington, worked out solutions to both problems. Butler developed a program to dam the rivers of flight flowing into Union encampments, punish Confederate planters, and propitiate the Unionists. Black people would continue to till the land of the Unionists, but as wage workers, provisioned with food, housing, and medical care, and protected from capital punishment by provost marshal officials.

Such officials would also direct wage laborers on abandoned plantations. General Banks, who replaced Butler in December 1862, coincident with the arrival of the Massachusetts 52nd, fine-tuned Butler's program and extended it to the rest of Louisiana. The recent Speaker of the House (and political chameleon) was still more inclined to mollify the Unionists, even as he reluctantly conceded that the fabric of the slave system was too tattered to be mended. Free labor would be encouraged, but only in name. Former enslaved people in the camps would continue to be treated as wage workers, but suspected vagrants and idlers would be rounded up and forced to work. Later, some would have to sign yearly contracts that stipulated payment in the form of small shares of the proceeds of the crop—anticipating the sharecropping system that would prevail throughout the region during Reconstruction and afterward. Hired Black workers, moreover, could not leave plantations without a pass. They could escape fieldwork, however, by seeking out army officials, who had been empowered by the Emancipation Proclamation and executive initiative to recruit regiments of Black soldiers. This initiative furthered heightened discord between the planters, whatever their loyalties, and the army.[29]

Banks's system, imposed as it was from above, would have been tough to enforce under any circumstances; the turmoil of war-torn Louisiana, in conjunction with the heterodox outlooks of subordinate officers, made it nearly impossible. Regimental leaders and provost marshal officials alike barraged Banks's secretaries with myriad questions. The general's program was not fully running in late January 1863, when a Vermont regimental captain wrote that several contraband, assured that they would be paid "$10 per month & rations" for harvesting the sugar, were left in the lurch. They had been paid earlier and most of them "can find employment if they have passes or some paper from an officer that will protect the Employer . . . and the contraband from arrest.—Several of whom have been arrested and made to pay a snug little sum for some purpose and then released." He asked Banks, "Have I any right or Authority to issue any sort of paper that will protect . . . Contraband . . . ? "[30] Later in the year, another officer wanted to know what to do with obstreperous "contraband " who left their plantations for his camp at Plaquemine. "How are these men to be treated?" he asked. "Are they to be returned to their Masters? If so, how is it to be done?" He ended by saying that he'd been told that "many of them desire to join a Colored Regiment."[31] Such units of the Louisiana Native Guards caused no end of headaches for Banks and his men. They were accused of everything—seemingly with some merit—from raiding smokehouses and stealing cordwood from plantations to inciting their people from the fields and cabins.[32]

Moreover, Black people sometimes displayed shocking militancy—and whites responded in kind. In early May a detachment of the 52nd that had been sent south of Baton Rouge got word of "trouble" between the Black and white populations near St. Martinsville. A captain of Company F, who took a group of thirty men to investigate and "secure the peace," arrived to find "great excitement."The "negroes had armed themselves, and were threatening the inhabitants with all manner of disaster." A "sharp skirmish" was said to have ensued, in which the whites "had the advantage, and secured ten of the leaders in the trouble. They then took to the bridge over the river, pinioned their arms and legs, placed a noose around the neck of each one, and at a given signal . . . left them dangling in the air," in what may have been one of the first mass lynchings in the South.[33] Two months later the African American press carried stories of massacres of Black fugitives and Black prisoners by Confederate troops in various parts of Louisiana.[34]

These dramatic episodes could not be confirmed, either in the mainstream press or in official Union army records. They occurred toward the end of Gere's and Stearns's service in the Massachusetts 52nd. However, months earlier, Gere had already seen enough of self-liberation and the disorder that ensued to give it a name. He called it "chaotic freedom"—an apt term indeed for the context in which he and his comrade served their country and its cause.[35]

Why did they enlist at all? It is easier to understand Henry S. Gere's motivation. He was both a devout Unionist and a firebrand abolitionist, someone with a long history of involvement, stretching back to his teenage years, in antislavery journalism and politics. The abolitionist master printer who directed Gere's apprenticeship left him with both a lifelong trade and an enduring commitment to emancipation and civil rights for Black people. He breathed abolitionist fervor into the three newspapers he published successively, from 1846 until his death in 1914. By turns he was a Liberty Party supporter before he was old enough to vote, then a Free Soiler, and finally a Republican, working for years as head of the Hampshire County organization. A principled and militant egalitarian, he welcomed African American speakers to town, drummed up attendance for their public lectures, and denounced white supremacy more broadly. His passion for equality extended to immigrants, for he was also an ardent anti-nativist who campaigned effectively to keep the local Republican organization free of the xenophobia that tarnished the party elsewhere. Answering a Know-Nothing initiative to strip foreigners of their right to vote, he thundered, "What! Proscribe a man through his whole life to a broader Americanism? We say . . . that a man who is an American in feeling, American in action . . . is an American."[36] The publisher also positioned himself at the center of the signal political dramas of the 1850s, devoting his papers to supporting local Black resistance to the Fugitive Slave Act in 1850, and in 1859 helping to arrange a memorial service for John Brown, a bold act that endeared him to the local Garrisonians but did not go down well with townies, who boycotted the event.[37]

For all his fierce antislavery militancy and noxious hatred of the South, Gere did not welcome war to preserve the Union and end slavery. He clung fast to futile hopes for a compromise, but when war did come he sought to democratize local support for the men at the front and their families at home. He joined with longtime abolitionist friends to advocate a war tax that would ensure that everyone did their part and pressed young men of the higher classes to sign up in order to broaden enlistment. By summer 1862 it was evident that he had faltered: the town rejected his fiscal plan, and enlistment numbers, though respectable, were not what he had wished. In addition, news of the Union disasters at Shiloh in April, followed by (the Second) Bull

FIGURE 2. Marshall S. Stearns in uniform at around age thirty-nine. Photo courtesy of the Northfield Historical Society, Northfield, Massachusetts.

Run in August, fell like a cold, hard rain on the town. It was in this context that Gere decided to take action, striding to the front of a town meeting and conspicuously signing his name to the muster roll, a huge personal step for a man of thirty-four but also a bit of theater contrived to arouse flagging morale for the Union and against slavery.[38]

Marshall Spring Stearns came from similar origins in western Massachusetts. His hometown of Northfield was more agricultural than Gere's birthplace, the industrializing Williamsburg, though like Williamsburg it bordered a county seat, in this case Greenfield, some twenty miles north of Northampton. Stearns's father was a house carpenter who built a successful business with his own brother and then his oldest sons. The elder Stearns was known by the War of 1812 as "Northfield's most prominent builder," and his sons extended his reputation, seeding the region with their signature Greek Revival houses. It was common for sons of men in the better trades to follow in the footsteps of their fathers, but Marshall Stearns, the eighth of ten children, went his own way. It is not possible to know why he did so, one of many questions surrounding a life we know only in broad outline.

Four years older than Gere, Stearns tried his hand at leatherwork, and then possibly farming, before turning to carpentry later in life. He attended the local common school and may have done a year at New Salem Academy, which gave him the equivalent of a modern high school education, but it made only a slight impression. He was articulate though not fully literate, splattering his letters (the only source we have from him) with misspellings and careless constructions. In 1850, against the wishes of his family, he joined fellow Yankees seeking the main chance in the California gold rush, but prospected in vain and turned either to outfitting the miners or farm management, possibly both. A life-changing opportunity came up by chance in early 1860, when his older brother died and the family farmstead passed to Charles, another house carpenter not eager to shift course. Marshall's sister-in-law got word to him at the end of the year that Charles considered "his trade . . . more congenial to him than farming" and offered the family house to him. Marshall wrote back in March, "I immediately made up my mind to go home. . . ."[39]

Not long after he got back from California, he married Sula Hillard, a schoolteacher from a Northfield family and possibly his childhood sweetheart.[40] The couple had three surviving girls; the first, Katie, was born two weeks after Stearns joined the Union army. Why would a new father of his age leave home—and for combat no less? We can rule out second thoughts over his marriage and doubts about parenthood; from the start of his service, he wrote home often and with unstinting, heartfelt love. In his first surviving letter, penned a week after he left New York for Louisiana in December 1862 (aboard the converted troop carrier *Illinois*), he told Sula, "When it is pleasant I wish you was with me & when it is rough I know you are better off at home. Keep of good cheer my Dear," ending, "If I live to come back you & I will go together . . . & live together as long as we are allowed to by him who rules all things well."[41] He was so starved for her that, as early as the middle of the month, he started counting the days until he returned—"six months & 22 days."[42] Several months later his letters came thicker and faster—and they were more passionate and guilt-ridden. Still counting the days, in March he wrote that he hoped it would be only three months before "I can take you in my arms & received [*sic*] one of your sweet kisses."[43] He gently chided her for failing to write often enough and expressed misgivings for being away and for not "helping you take care of our little Katie that I long to see."[44] By the end of April, his spirits were higher, and he reminded Sula that he would be home in "two months and thirteen days." "PS," he signed off, "a kiss for you and Katie."[45]

Stearns was a considerate husband as well as a loving one. In March he wrote Sula that he had been offered "a major commission in the engineering corps," a post he had not sought but a tempting one indeed, given its generous salary of $189 a month—nearly ten times the pay of an ordinary soldier, a sum tidy enough to float a solidly middle-class style of life. He reckoned that it would "support" them in comfort, leave something for a cushy retirement, and sustain their "Mutual good."[46] He mulled over the offer for a day or two and decided to reject the position because it did not come with the benefit of time off. "I want [to] see our little darling so much," he told Sula, "that I would not take [the] Col Commission" without a promise of a furlough.[47] A month later he turned down still another promotion, this time, he said, because he preferred to "go with the men I know"—i.e., those from his own regiment—and we can safely assume that the question of additional time away from his family also figured into his decision.[48] Within a week he fired off two letters to Sula, complaining that he had not heard from her and that he wished he were by her side in order to hold up his end of familial responsibility.[49]

The cipher in this tender correspondence is Sula. Her views on race and slavery before her marriage are no clearer to us than his. Northfield hosted two branches of the American Antislavery Society in the late 1830s, with a total of ninety members, a fairly strong following for a village of fewer than a thousand people.[50] But at present it is impossible to tell whether Marshall or Sula joined the group or supported one of the town's antislavery parties. We are left with two possibilities. One is that Stearns began his service as a Unionist, not as an antislavery man. We know that he was insistent about enlisting, not only because of the timing of it, but also because he helped recruit Company F for the Massachusetts 52nd, a chore that earned him the rank of lieutenant.[51] His Unionism seems to have resembled that of James K. Hosmer, the Deerfield cleric who served in Company D of the 52nd. In his memoir, Hosmer asserted that he "believed in the war from the first," but not a war for emancipation. He expressed thinly veiled cynicism regarding the enslaved people, explaining that "my sympathies go as much or more with the suffering whites than the suffering blacks."[52] "The cause of the North, briefly, is to me, the cause of civilization and liberty."[53] He would put his life on the line for the Union, but for nothing more.

Though Stearns never mentioned devotion to the Union in his brief surviving correspondence with his family, he hinted at sharing Hosmer's reverent patriotism by alternately referring to the Southern foe as "traitors," "cursed traitors," and so forth.[54] He also implied in his earliest letters that it was Sula who bore the abolitionist flag. As the steamer that transported the 52nd from New York dropped anchor within eyeshot of New Orleans in mid-December 1862, he wrote his wife that it would have been a "great treat" to have had her by his side and a "pleasure" for her to have seen more than the "fine orchards of oranges." She also would have appreciated the enthusiastic welcome from Black individuals gathered on the riverbank at the edge of the city. It was quite a sight, he wrote, to witness the "darkey's swing their Hats bonnets Handkerchiefs & . . . jump & turn around & jump again. . . ."[55]

He came around in part because of his own reckoning with slavery, Louisiana style. A month into his hitch, he referred to a "Niger" regiment that came through his area and noted with irritation that he had been put in charge of the "contrabands" in Baton Rouge. He guessed that his friends back home would "laugh & sneer when they hear that I have charge of the contrabands; that will not hurt me this far off." He assured her that "my opinion is just the same now in respects to Nigers as it was when I left home. . . ."—implying that he was a racist.[56] Not long afterward, however, his language and attitude softened; he stopped referring to Black people as "Nigers" in favor of the milder epithet of "darkeys," and he increasingly used the more respectful descriptive "negro." Though at first he tried repeatedly to be relieved of his duties with the contrabands, he eventually accepted the post and performed responsibly. By the end of January 1863, he even distanced himself from fellow officers who had groused about the appearance of a "darkey" regiment, commenting that he thought they "drill as well as we did" and he took the unpopular position that, if it were up to him, he would "let them fight."[57]

Stearns's devotion to the well-being of his men, obvious from the start of the war, strengthened in the course of the conflict. By March the local hospital overflowed with soldiers suffering from wounds and fever and turned away many more queueing for medical attention. Stearns wrote his mother, in a matter-of-fact way, that his position "has been an advantage to some of the boys as I have saved them from going into a hospital by taking them [to my house to nurse,] as I would like to have [them] do for me under like circumstances."[58] His position also proved to be an advantage for the contrabands under his charge. His compound, a converted female seminary on the edge of the city, saw its population rise from some four hundred runaways in mid-December to over a thousand at the end of the month, and it would soon soar to two thousand (with about three thousand more located on nearby plantations run by his staff).[59] (See figure 3.) Some of the runaways arrived in the most horrid

FIGURE 3. "Headquarters of 1st Contraband Camp, Baton Rouge, La." Marshall Dunham photograph album, Louisiana State University Libraries Special Collections, Baton Rouge.

conditions—weakened, famished, and dressed in rags or, as he wrote his mother, "nearly naked."[60] He had to feed and clothe them and also transfer the able-bodied men (and perhaps some women) to the government-run plantations. He not only organized a massive commissary, he also managed to distribute crude shoes and thousands of yards of cloth for sewing into garments.[61]

Though deeply moved by the pathetic and squalid state of his charges, it was the question of color that shook his conscience. He immediately noticed that not all contrabands had dark skin, writing in early January that some 1,250 had come into his camp. It was a "sight to behold," from the "real Africans to the 7/8 children with light hare & blue eyes and fair complection," who to his amazement "are Slaves."[62] He earlier wrote Sula that he had his own "waiter," a "slave but he is so white that you would not dream that his mother was anything less than a white woman."[63] The spectacle of a white enslaved person unnerved him, and as a modern scholar has observed, he "struggled" with the question of slavery, race, and race mixing. Not a particularly reflective man, "he never arrived at a coherent understanding of the social and cultural understanding of a 'white nigger.'"[64] What he did do was evolve from an ignorant and naïve racist—someone who had never seen an African American, much less known one—into a more enlightened man. The decency that he displayed to fellow soldiers in need deepened, broadened, and informed his understanding of the fundamental personhood of Black individuals. His war for the Union pivoted into a war for emancipation.

Greater and greater numbers of enslaved people certainly read it that way, further confirming Henry Gere's idea of "chaotic freedom." They continued to flee their plantations in late March as detachments from the 52nd Regiment marched southwest from Baton Rouge en route to Port Hudson. Terrified planters lit out across the Red River into Texas, with their enslaved people in tow or on their own, leaving the fields in the hands of their laborers. In early April, a former sergeant in the Confederate army showed up in camp in the guise of an agent; the fugitive he came to claim had by then become the servant of a regimental officer. His request divided the regiment and nearly caused a gunfight; as the men squared off, the enslaved-person-turned-servant fled into the woods. In response, the commanding officer of the brigade ordered all officers to "return within twenty-four hours to the provost-marshal all negroes who have come into the line since Donaldsville," a village forty miles south of Baton Rouge. The order "perplexed" Colonel Halbert Greenleaf, the commander of the 52nd and a very popular figure. The regimental chaplain explained that Greenleaf felt it was "perfectly unjust" for him to "call in the whole regiment to aid, in restoring fugitives"; at the same time, he could not be sure that the higher-ups intended to "return these men to their masters."[65] At the end of the month Greenleaf got a visit from "a delegation of negroes—intelligent, healthy, hearty-looking fellows" who came to "advise me on the situation." He inquired "whence they came and to whom they belonged. They answered that they came from a plantation about two miles away belonging to 'Massa Gantt,'—our Union friend and planter." He asked if Gantt was "kind to them. They said that he was. If he fed and clothed them well[?] They said he did; they had no fault whatever to find with his treatment of them, but 'they wanted to be free.'" Greenleaf was moved, but not enough to take their side, and ordered them "to remain, for the present, just where they were." A few weeks later at Gantt's plantation he saw "some of the negroes again—saw how they fared, how they lived, etc—and was confirmed in the opinion that I had given wise counsel."[66] The men continued to be treated well, he surmised, but the fact is that they remained in bondage.

In areas slipping away from Confederate control, efforts to resolve the muddle over the status of fugitives sometimes proved as effective as consulting the entrails of a sacrificial sheep. In late April, Augustus B. Long—a captain in the 52nd and provost marshal in the tumultuous environs of St. Martin's Parish (where the status of the Emancipation Proclamation was debatable)—appealed to the provost marshal general for guidance. Long explained that he had previously "encouraged the idea of freedom among slaves not anticipating the exemption of this Parish" from the Emancipation Proclamation, and was now at a loss. "What policy," he asked, "shall be pursued now towards the hundred who came flocking in here[?] Are they to be advised to return to their masters or compelled[?]" The following day he issued a circular asserting that the "generally received impression" that the "slaves of this Parish, are free by the presence of the Union army, is *erroneous,*" because the parish was in fact "excepted" from the president's historic executive order. The circular went on to proclaim that the army would countenance "no further interference" with slavery in the parish, but would also not return fugitives to their masters, except for those who went back "voluntarily." The army would protect such fugitives from abuse and also "arrest" masters who "used force" to capture their runaways. A week later he appealed again to his superior for clarification in a cover letter that included the circular—but never received a response.[67]

In striking contrast, Stearns erred on the side of leniency. Unlike his own commanding officer, it appears that he never consulted his provost marshal for guidance or clarification; indeed, he never even mentioned such an official in his correspondence to his wife or mother. His early letters indicate that he made his own decisions from the first, exploiting the leeway in the administrative confusion. In early January he told Sula that his unexpected role as Superintendent of Negro Labor saddled him with a "big job" that sometimes left him grumpy, such that he "growl[ed] some of the time." Yet he remained clear-headed enough when it came to dealing with "Secesh gents and women when they want their slaves back." "I go to the Quarters," he explained, and "let them pick them out," without bothering to ask whether they were pro-Union or not.

Stearns describes what typically follows: "They make speeches about no one to help them, and then I say [to the runaways,] 'Do you want to go home with her?' The answer is "No' in every case. The negro says she has been abused and . . . stripped her shoulder bare to the hide (as they term it) and took 20 to 40 stripes. I listen a minute and then tell the secesh sister that she cannot have her servant. This happens over and over."[68]

The record is sketchy thereafter, but there is no evidence that Stearns ever toed the line drawn by more literal-minded officers. The telltale signs of abuse, which he saw for himself early on, stayed with him for the rest of the conflict.

THE ABOLITIONIST HENRY S. GERE came with a more sophisticated perspective to his wartime service. Not only better educated and more politically aware than Stearns, he was also an innovative journalist and had made news gathering a central feature of his Northampton newspapers. Gere brought his sharp eye and a nose for the news to his stint for the 52nd. Well over six feet tall, his age, literacy, and commanding presence underwrote his stature with his men and likely explained his promotion to postmaster. We know of his wartime experience not through personal correspondence, but from letters he wrote to his *Hampshire*

FIGURE 4. Henry S. Gere. This is one of only two known images of Gere; there are none of him in uniform. In this photograph he is probably around age seventy. Courtesy of Forbes Library, Northampton, Massachusetts.

Gazette—roughly two a month—from November 1862 until the following August, when he completed his service. He intended to keep the home front informed of the meaning of war; his letters, unlike Stearns's, were for public consumption, at once critical and didactic.

Gere commented liberally on numerous aspects of the war. One of his commanders, playfully if derisively, called his 52nd a "schoolmaster regiment," as if to say that it lacked the toughness of the more hardened, three-year enlistees.[69] The postmaster shared this point of view and added his own note of skepticism. He was a grown man among "young men—mere boys . . . three-quarters of them . . . under 22 years of age." It was an "outrage" to send such callow youths to war. It made more sense to increase the age of enlistment to twenty-five, drawing upon more mature and stronger men, troops who might show better judgment and greater resistance to disease.[70]

He was no easier on the military hierarchy. Life aboard the *Illinois* was "monotonous and tedious" and also irritating because of the palpable distinction "between the officers and the privates that disheartens me more than anything else." The brass at "one end of the ship" enjoyed "all the luxuries of a hotel," while the enlisted men "at the other end [were] furnished only with the coarsest, necessaries of life, illy cooked [food] and . . . denied the privilege of even buying from the ship's steward a piece of fresh bread, a cup of tea . . . a wholesomely cooked mouthful of any sort." In addition, they were "stowed away in close quarters in a place your south street farmers would no more think of stalling their cattle than they would of knocking them in the head in the street." It was no wonder that the "private soon comes to feel that he is degraded," but also a tribute to them that "many return to their homes with characters so good."[71] He later complained of poor training, noting that after a couple of weeks in Baton Rouge, the men drilled but had no schooling in marksmanship despite the fact that "no small number . . . [had] never loaded or fired a gun."[72]

Gere's appointment as postmaster made him especially popular. Postal officials were the candy men of the war; they delivered the sweetness of letters and newspapers from the home front, along with packages of every imaginable comfort—from pillows and blankets to barrels of Connecticut Valley apples and quarts of maple syrup. Gere soon found himself schooling the raw and jejune recruits. Not long after his company settled into Baton Rouge, he decided "'to show the boys how to cook,' and to their astonishment and delight, a huge pile of fried pork, fried hard tack, and fried potatoes began to show itself."[73] Once he became postmaster, he left behind tent, campfire, and drilling field for more refined living, moving into a building formally occupied by the commander in charge of the U.S. arsenal. It was a "commodious" structure with high ceilings, "well furnished rooms, coal grates, marble arch frames, elegant piazzas, [and] brick walks." He and his fellow officers had their own cook, a runaway, who made sure they had "no difficulty satisfying the calls of hunger."[74]

Yet Gere was no homebody, content to bask in the perquisites of office. The episodic work of sorting and distributing the mail left him with quite a bit of time to wander around

Baton Rouge and ponder what this gruesome war was all about—occasions to get to know African Americans, and not simply the abstraction of slavery, that consuming cause of his civilian years. In early February, he exclaimed, "Can't think of anything, except the everlasting and ever present negro. My God, what a people!" and then asked, "What is the world to him, or he to the world? What are his hopes, and what his aspirations? . . . What shall become of him?"[75] "The Negro," he reflected at the end of the month, "is a great study," and he wrote, in a palpable change of heart, "I am glad I came here, in spite of the villainous voyage, so pregnant with death, if for no other reason than the opportunity . . . to see the negroes as they are—the good, the bad, and the indifferent—on the soil which they till and curse. No one can know them by hearsay, or by reading. They must be seen, watched, studied . . . to be fully understood and their condition fully appreciated."[76]

Gere nonetheless refrained from treating the Black people he encountered as specimens. Apart from his personal servant, he befriended none of them, but made a point of finding out how they felt about their condition and their prospects. He went out of his way to engage them, talking at length to the beleaguered fugitives at the contraband camp, around town, on nearby plantations, and also at local Black chapels. It goes without saying that most of his fellow white soldiers were markedly less adventurous and forthcoming. Racist to begin with, they were repulsed by the unwashed and ragged runaways pouring into their lines. The overwhelming majority went through the war with not so much as a word with a Black Louisianan. Gere was determined to correct popular misconceptions about the Southern Black population.

Though Gere was as astonished as Stearns by the gradations of skin color in Louisiana, unlike Stearns he paused to think about the implications of race mixing. He observed "a large proportion of yellow faces" milling about Stearns's contraband camp.[77] Gere later wrote that his close-up study of slavery "does not produce any liking for it. We see the pale faces of the mulattoes, and laugh at the Southern talk of 'Yankee amalgamation.'" Race mixing was "one of the most peculiar of the many peculiarities of this peculiar institution." It was not "Yankee blood either," but the blood of debauched masters who preyed upon their female property, he correctly commented.[78] The fact that some sexual unions produced children who were "nearly white" yet remained in chains startled Gere and served as a still another indictment of the master class, a class so craven and morally disfigured that it enslaved its own children. What else did the critics of abolitionism need to know?

Gere also perceived social distinctions within Black Louisiana that escaped most Yankee observers. The preponderance of the fugitives was composed of "field hands," but he noticed that "there are among them quite a number of mechanics, who are intelligent and smart." One had come "all the way from Jackson, Miss., about 60 miles distant. Good for him," he wrote in admiration.[79] No Black men impressed him more than those who passed on intelligence or suited up for the army. He told of one crafty Black man—owned by a Confederate sympathizer—who "quietly and stealthily started for the Union camp, where we have information he possessed. A cavalry force was forthwith sent out, the negro leading the way, and the rebel [was] captured. He is now in our hands, a prisoner of war. The negro remained on the plantation as if nothing happened . . . ready to improve the next opportunity."[80]

Gere once confessed that he had had to be convinced of the wisdom of recruiting Black troops, but that appears to have been a tactical denial. The fact is that, even as he regretted the "general prejudice against them in the army," he was impressed with them from the first time he saw a regiment of the Louisiana Native Guards in late February 1863.[81] A month later he continued to deplore the low "expectations from the negroes"; he himself admired their "good appearance on parade" and believed they "will fight if called to it," just as Stearns had said.[82] When they were called upon to lay siege to the rebel encampment at Port Hudson, Gere provided a favorable report, one that studiously avoided the racially tinged metaphors of other accounts—those that likened the heroic soldiers to "tigers"—that is, to animals. The Black regiments, he wrote, "acquitted themselves nobly. Their most ardent friends," he supposed, "could not have expected more from them."[83]

What did Black people want? What did they expect from the war? These were the key questions for Gere; he visited them again and again, but not without some evidence for himself and his readers. His clearest statement on the matter came in the course of a church service he witnessed, presided over by a white captain. Following the officer's "earnest prayer," the "negroes all kneeled, and responded with supplications" and then united in a hymn that evoked "emotions . . . in the greatest degree. With hands uplifted and eyes closed, they entered into the singing with an enthusiasm such as I had never beheld before." When the service ended, he approached several of them to find out why they had left their masters, asking if they "were not better off where they were, & c." They generally said they were "well off enough, 'but we want to be free.'" This "instinct of love for freedom," he stressed, was "very strong." Yet he was not wide-eyed or uncritical, writing that the prevailing notion of freedom was " not very intelligent." They believe they "will not have to work, will have fine houses . . . good clothes to wear," but when told that they "will have to work harder than when at home, that they will have no better clothes, and no better places to live, they say 'we know we' among friends."[84]

Gere did not sugarcoat the fate of newly freed Black people. He knew "they must be taken care of. How is the question. It is a great, a mighty work, but still imperious. We cannot escape it if we would, and ought not if we could." He took the long and sagacious view, explaining to his readers that it would take the best efforts "of this and the succeeding generations simply because there was no easy solution." He advised that we "must feel our way . . . have patience . . . exercise fortitude . . . , nourish charity. Errors will be made—they are unavoidable—but this work will go on, and in the process of time . . . this unfortunate race, now so reduced in the scale of humanity, will be improved, and this nation, now so severely tried by bad men and bad elements . . . shall shine forth as brightly as its institutions are glorious and priceless."[85]

Stearns and Gere probably met for the first time in the fall during basic training at Camp Miller in Greenfield, Massachusetts. Gere knew Stearns well enough by late December to think of him as "just the man for the position" of head of the contrabands, without explaining what he meant.[86] They became close associates, if not friends, men who left behind records of two mutual experiences—telling collaborations on behalf of runaways.

One of these occurred at the end of June, when Stearns took Gere on a routine inspection of the plantations under his command. "It seemed good once more," Gere wrote, "to ride in a respectable vehicle" because he had earlier been confined to a hospital bed for a few weeks with a fever. He welcomed the chance to get out of Baton Rouge, share time with his colleague, and see Stearns's charges for himself. The plantations were huge operations, with about a thousand workers each, far larger than the surrounding spreads. They were still in civilian hands and mostly devoted to raising foodstuffs for the workers and the elderly men, women, and children in the contraband camps.

Gere gave the plantations a mixed assessment, observing that no one expected the fields of wheat and sweet potatoes to turn a profit. The real "benefits are the employment of a large number of negroes in a manner that enables them to partially support themselves." They could not fully support themselves because of the pitiful wages, nor were they fully free or completely secure. Quite apart from their immobility, they were vulnerable to con men and hucksters angling to cheat them out of a few dollars, as well as the agents of planters and bounty hunters out to re-enslave them. Gere saw the danger firsthand when Stearns's subordinates apprehended a few "secest't citizens" on suspicion "of being engaged in a scheme to molest our men"—presumably to trick some field workers into returning to their masters. They were questioned and then released "on their good behavior." Gere wrote that they would "conduct themselves properly" only if "they fear [the] cold lead and steel" of the Union army, a point he would stress many times over when his service ended.[87]

Two months earlier the pair had also collaborated in the making of an image of a badly abused enslaved man, a portrait widely known today as Peter. A compelling piece of abolitionist propaganda, the image quickly became iconic, circulating throughout the South and then the entire nation. It long survived the bloody conflict, rather like the searing photograph of the "Napalm Girl" from the Vietnam War. Generations of Americans have seen the image of Peter in U.S. history texts, museum exhibitions, television specials, as well as on websites. Recently a cable news network—while covering the gruesome murder of nine African Americans at a Bible class in the Emmanuel Methodist Episcopal Church in Charleston, South Carolina—superimposed the image of Peter on a picture of the church. Apparently, no treatment of Southern slavery and the Civil War, or even a current civil rights story, is complete without Peter.

The photograph, taken in Baton Rouge in early April 1863, was sent not long afterward to *Harper's Weekly,* which published it in a special edition on July 4, accompanied by a narrative. The *Harper's* article included an eye-catching woodcut based on three original photos, a

July 4, 1863.] HARPER'S WEEKLY. 429

RAID OF SECOND SOUTH CAROLINA VOLUNTEERS (COL. MONTGOMERY) AMONG THE RICE PLANTATIONS ON THE COMBAHEE, S. C.—[See Page 427.]

A TYPICAL NEGRO.

We publish herewith three portraits, from photographs by M'Pherson and Oliver, of the negro Gordon, who escaped from his master in Mississippi, and came into our lines at Baton Rouge in March last. One of these portraits represents the man as he entered our lines, with clothes torn and covered with mud and dirt from his long race through the swamps and bayous, chased as he had been for days and nights by his master with several neighbors and a pack of blood-hounds; another shows him as he underwent the surgical examination previous to being mustered into the service—his back furrowed and scarred with the traces of a whipping administered on Christmas-day last; and the third represents him in United States uniform, bearing the musket and prepared for duty.

This negro displayed unusual intelligence and energy. In order to foil the scent of the blood-hounds who were chasing him he took from his plantation onions, which he carried in his pockets. After crossing each creek or swamp he rubbed his body freely with these onions, and thus, no doubt, frequently threw the dogs off the scent.

At one time in Louisiana he served our troops as guide, and on one expedition was unfortunately taken prisoner by the rebels, who, infuriated beyond measure, tied him up and beat him, leaving him for dead. He came to life, however, and once more made his escape to our lines.

By way of illustrating the degree of brutality which slavery has developed among the whites in the section of country from which this negro came, we append the following extract from a letter in the New York Times, recounting what was told by the refugees from Mrs. Gillespie's estate on the Black River:

GORDON AS HE ENTERED OUR LINES.

GORDON UNDER MEDICAL INSPECTION.

GORDON IN HIS UNIFORM AS A U. S. SOLDIER.

FIGURE 5. Page from *Harper's Weekly,* July 4, 1863. Wood engraving. National Portrait Gallery, Smithsonian Institution.

triptych with Peter (renamed Gordon) in the center, stripped to the waist to expose his lurid back, and flanked by two images: one of him in rags as he entered the Union lines and the other of him wearing Union blue. The accompanying narrative, "A Typical Slave," indicated that Peter had been beaten at a Mississippi plantation the previous Christmas and then escaped, making his way to Baton Rouge through perseverance and guile, having rubbed himself with onions to befuddle the hounds of his pursuers. Nursed back to health by Union physicians, he joined the army as a scout, only to be captured by Confederates, beaten yet again, and left for dead. Nevertheless he survived and returned to his Union friends, serving the cause with distinction.[88]

This gripping narrative and its striking images captivated a Northern public still skeptical of the Emancipation Proclamation and smarting from the recent battlefield defeats. Even *Harper's,* which had begun to doubt the war, now reversed course and declared the conflict worthwhile after all. It considered Peter's scars to be emblematic of Southern barbarism and further underlined his obvious suffering, claiming that enslaved people like him were brutalized not only by the whip but also tortured with "hot embers on their back."[89] The *Liberator* carried letters from Union officers testifying that he was one of "hundreds of such sights."[90] Modern scholars agree that this was an astonishingly effective piece of pro-war hype, one that circulated beyond the kinetic abolitionist circuit to the wider public.[91] It represented, writes a contemporary thinker, "the promise of manhood and citizenship for black men who enlisted to fight for the Union."[92]

New photographic technology made the pictures of Peter possible. The civilian population thirsted for war news in print, and especially for images from the bloody battlefront. Yet the old photographic form of the daguerreotype did not easily lend itself to outdoor photography and proved nearly impossible to reproduce—or share. Invented in 1839 and wildly popular as a means of portraiture, daguerreotypes were quickly displaced on the eve of the Civil War by the wet-plate collodion process, which produced a negative image. The negative could then be used to make either another negative image (ambrotype) or a positive print (carte de visite) which was mounted on card stock, typically two and a half by four inches, roughly similar to modern-day postcards.

These *cartes*—cheap to produce (about fifty cents each) and reproduce—were major advances over the old technology. They soon became the rage. "Cartomania," as it was called, was fueled by soldiers mugging for the camera and eager for mementos of their wartime experience. Military men from both sides traded them as eagerly as youths in post–World War II America collected and traded the pictures of sports icons and celebrities wrapped in chewing gum packages. Gere himself, as noted above, joined in the craze, accumulating cartes de visite of fellow soldiers, African Americans, and street scenes, not only of Baton Rouge but other sites in the South. His legacy of Civil War mementos includes another image of Stearns's contraband camp, a poignant reminder of his political commitments and wartime experiences.[93] Since they could be easily mailed back home, friends and families multiplied the

FIGURE 6. "Contraband Yard, formerly used as a Female Seminary." G. H. Suydam photograph album. Louisiana State University Libraries Special Collections, Baton Rouge.

demand for such collectibles.[94] And thus Peter's image became widely known in the North.

But was the *Harper's* narrative authentic? The historian David Silkenat casts serious doubt on this stirring story. Through a careful analysis of overlooked sources, Silkenat argues that "there is good evidence to suggest" that the magazine's copy "was largely fabricated and [that] much of what we know about 'Gordon' may be inaccurate."[95] He shows that the author, Vincent Colyer, motivated by his own abolitionist convictions, invented Peter's courage and valor. In addition, two images that flanked Peter were fallacious: the Black man in tattered clothing was not Peter, and neither was the other man in Union blue. *Harper's* never bothered to check the accuracy of Colyer's story or the authenticity of the accompanying illustrations. It was a matter of converging interests—between a politically motivated author and an overly enthusiastic publication keen to scoop its rivals.[96]

Silkenat also maintains that there were at least three photographs of Peter, two taken in early April, about a week after he arrived in Baton Rouge, and a third taken at the end of April. In the first two photos, his hair is closely cropped, except for a telltale peak on the top of his head; in the third image, Peter leans farther to the left, a pose arranged by the photographer in order to reveal more of his lacerated back and magnify the effect of his wounds. In the words of a modern scholar, the craft of "provocative . . . lighting, careful positioning, thoughtful lines and contours" made for an "overall powerful composition" and "commanding anti-slavery image."[97] This last image is the escaped enslaved man whom *Harper's* would rechristen "Gordon" and who appeared in the center of the triptych. It is also the portrait that is best known, having effectively displaced the other pictures of Peter taken in early April.[98]

Further evidence for Peter's identity, and for *Harper's* inaccuracies, comes from a self-described "Bostonian" writing in the *New York Tribune* in December 1863, after the widespread reaction to the *Harper's* piece. He asserted that

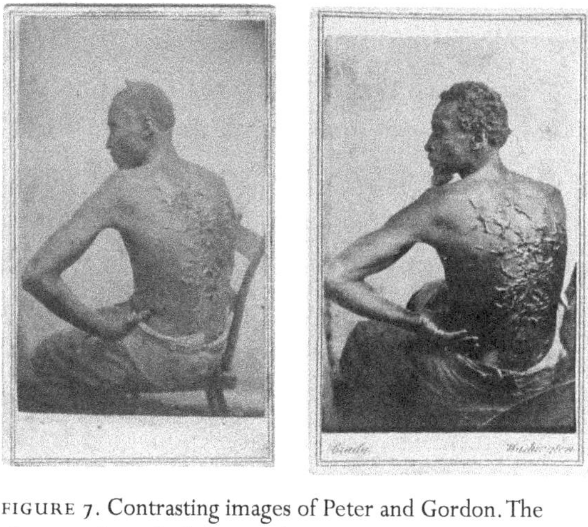

FIGURE 7. Contrasting images of Peter and Gordon. The photograph on the left was taken in early April, the one on the right later that month. Courtesy National Portrait Gallery, Smithsonian Institution.

the previous summer he had sent *Harper's* photographs of four fugitives who ran off together. One was sent to scavenge for food for the group but was apparently recaptured and murdered. Of the three who made it to the Union lines, one was named Peter and another was named Gordon. They were different men. Gordon appeared in the left side of the *Harper's* triptych, dressed in rags, barefoot, and wearing a weathered hat with a brim.[99] He was not, as *Harper's* wrote, the man depicted in the center of the triptych—that man was Peter.

Who was Peter? "Bostonian" wrote that Peter, the runaway with "the lacerated back," was a French speaker who "spoke little English" and that he had to be questioned by Union officers in his native tongue. When asked why he had run away, he pulled away the "pile of dirty rags that half-concealed his back" and "exhibited his mutilated sable."[100] Additional details in "Bostonian's" account are confirmed by an interview of Peter at the studio of his Baton Rouge photographer, dated April 2, in which Peter explained that he was the enslaved of Captain John Lyon, a planter from Atchafalaya, near Washington, Louisiana. Lyon's overseer, Artayon Carrier, had administered the terrible beating "two months before Christmas," for reasons that remain unclear. Carrier may well have cooked up the excuse that Peter was "sort of crazy" and tried to "shoot everyone." "They told me so," Peter said to the Union authorities who ministered to him, but his wife said afterward that he "no do such things."[101] The fact is that Peter ran off in October, amid the rush of the harvest, a particularly bold act that would have provoked punishment well beyond the Louisiana shirt. In this case, it got Peter a furious beating, one that left him incapacitated for two months and then led him to bolt to Baton Rouge, where he finally landed in late March.

Who, then, was responsible for making these images? There is strong evidence that it was Gere and Stearns. We cannot say with absolute certainty, because Stearns's surviving letters contain no photographs of his wartime service. Gere's photographic legacy of thirty-three cartes de visite includes one image of two Black youths, presumably fugitives, and another of fugitives at a contraband camp.[102]

The remaining two images—one of a Black man in ragged clothing and the other of a Black soldier—are the portraits that flanked Peter in the triptych. But oddly enough, there is no Peter.

Instead, we must rely upon the written record, a record that points to Gere and Stearns. In a letter written on April 6, Gere explained that he "saw last week one of the most horrid and singular objects I have ever beheld. It was the bare back of a negro who had been beaten by an overseer." The lashing, which had been administered in the fall, left his back "a complete mass of blisters, the sight of which could hardly fail to make one shudder." Then he added, "Lieutenant Stearns took him to an artist and had a picture made of his back."[103] A week later Stearns told his wife in his colloquial style, "I will send you a fotergraf of a whipped darkey that came into my camp; you can have some idea of the looks of the poor fellow"[104] Two days later he wrote to his "Best Friend" that "I scent a Fotergraf of . . . [an enslaved person who] has been was whipped about the first half of November to my wife. It was such a horrid sight that I would have a picture of it [so] you aught to see it." He continued, "I will send you one of two ragged ones that came in to the Qtrs. have had some worse than rag[g]ed for I have had one come on that had nothing on." About to say more, Stearns was then interrupted by a telegram about "our forces" on the march to Port Hudson and abruptly ended his letter.[105]

Another piece of evidence also indicates that it was Peter they had in mind. An assistant surgeon with the Massachusetts 47th Regiment sent a "Colonel" the carte de visite of an enslaved man; the inscription on the reverse side reads, "I have found a large number of the four hundred contrabands examined by me to be as badly lacerated as the specimen [r]epresented in the enclosed photograph."[106] The picture is of Peter and the card is dated April 2, which is consistent with the dates of the letters written by Gere and Stearns, and with the interview of Peter mentioned above. In short, it is safe to assume that they were responsible for the original photograph of Peter. Multiple copies were soon made by photographers in New York and other urban studios, but it was the later picture of "Gordon," taken at the end of April and published by *Harper's,* that became the iconic image. The reason is clear enough. Gere and Stearns sent copies to a limited circle—Stearns to family and friends, and Gere to S. E. Bridgeman, a Northampton abolitionist who, he wrote, "will show it to anyone desiring to see it."[107] Gere and Stearns were modest men from rural western Massachusetts with comparatively limited horizons, not urban sophisticates, and it did not occur to them to seek a broader audience, nor, it seems, to embellish Peter's story. As Gere tersely put it, the original photograph "speaks for itself"—still more confirmation of the power of images to this Civil War generation that other observers confirmed.[108] Thus a Northern journalist, one of the first persons in his region to see the image, commented, "It tells a story the way that even Mrs. Stowe cannot approach, because it tells the story to the eye."[109] It is unlikely that he and his colleagues received their copies of Peter's portrait from Gere or Stearns. It is virtually certain that whoever sent it north was a more savvy actor, someone plugged into the

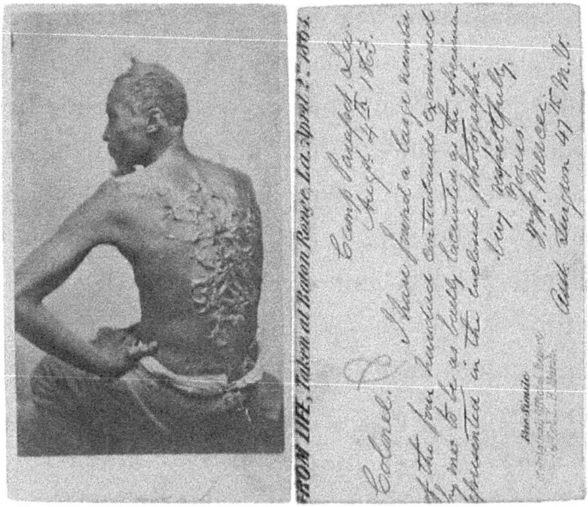

FIGURE 8. F. W. Mercer, assistant surgeon with the Massachusetts 47th Volunteers, sent this carte de visite with the appended note to a superior officer on or about the day that Stearns took Peter to a Baton Rouge "artist" to have his picture taken. Courtesy of the author.

region's abolitionist circles and leading media circuits as well.[110]

Indeed, William Lloyd Garrison's *Liberator* carried an advertisement for two months offering single copies of a carte de visite of Peter for fifteen cents and seven copies for a dollar.[111] It was this kind of publicity that made the third image of Peter the famous portrait.

So how can we account for the third image of Peter, taken in late April, in which he has a fuller head of hair and is renamed Gordon by *Harper's?* It is unlikely that he sought out a photographer on his own. Either someone took him to a photographer or one sought him out. Neither Stearns nor Gere mentioned a third sitting at a studio, nor did any other soldier in their unit, to my knowledge. Silence among the sources thus takes us to the irresolute terrain of inference and speculation. Two clear possibilities are the Union medics who treated Peter in Stearns's contraband camp. F. W. Mercer (sometimes misidentified as J. W. Mercer), an assistant surgeon with the 47th Massachusetts Volunteers, examined Peter when he arrived at the camp and, as we have already seen, wrote that he had observed a "large number" of runaways similarly brutalized.[112] The other medic was S. K. Towle, a surgeon with the 30th Regiment of the Massachusetts Volunteers, who also examined Peter and who described him as "INTELLIGENT and WELL BEHAVED."[113] Both officers might have been motivated to take Peter back to the photographer in late April for the sitting that further dramatized his scars—but whether they did so isn't at all clear.

Perhaps no officer accompanied Peter to the studio of William D. McPherson and J. Oliver in the center of Baton Rouge, the photographers credited with taking the first two pictures of Peter. We know nothing of Oliver and only a bit more of McPherson, but what we do know is intriguing. McPherson was born in 1833 in Boston and died in New Orleans in 1867, possibly in a yellow fever epidemic that swept through the Crescent City and put a premium on burying the dead as quickly as possible (and, alas, without obituaries). He had opened a studio in New Hampshire in 1856 and eventually followed the Union army to Baton Rouge, where he set up shop with Oliver in 1862, then moved to New Orleans in 1864.[114] McPherson's surviving portfolio of 124 images indicates that he worked from his studio and also (like many fellow artists) roamed the country as a camp follower, trekking along with Banks's army from Baton Rouge to New Orleans and from Donaldsville to Port Hudson and then the Red River Valley. While in the capital he photographed the huge Union encampment, the old arsenal grounds (where Gere was holed up), the town streets, and so forth; on the road he made numerous images of Confederate battlements, most famously a major series of pictures of Port Hudson.[115]

For our purposes, four images stand out. One shows a sugar plantation, another the enslaved people's huts on it or on another estate. A third, entitled "Men lined up outdoors," is blurry but may show newly freed men mustering for fieldwork. The final photograph, clearly one of several he made is labeled "Contraband Headquarters, Baton Rouge" or "1st Contraband Camp, Baton Rouge, La." It depicts a two-story building with porches on both levels. White men in Union blue pose casually on the top level, above a group of Black women and children.[116] This carte de visite and another shown earlier provide different views of Stearns's contraband camp, a place McPherson knew well and evidently thought worthy of multiple shots. Why take such images? Civil War photographers like McPherson chased the dollar, showing views of ships, encampments, battlefields strewn with the dead, and so forth. In the North there was also a market for McPherson's images of African Americans among the relatively small group of abolitionists and extending to the larger community of curious Yankees eager to know what the war was all about. But money may not have been his primary motivator. He may have taken such photographs out of conviction, born from the same concrete experiences with slavery that moved Stearns and other soldiers. If so, he would have needed no encouragement from Union officers to redo the image of Peter; he could well have taken it on his own.

HENRY GERE AND MARSHALL STEARNS returned from the war together with the rest of the Massachusetts 52nd, first by steamboat up the Mississippi River, then by train across the Midwest and through southern New England, stopping first in Gere's Northampton and then in Greenfield, not far from Stearns's Northfield. They were greeted by garlands, roses, and songs, with the local band playing the old favorite "Home, Sweet Home." The

52nd's homecoming was not so sweet for the father of one soldier, who expected to see his son but learned that the boy had died "on the day he was to start home."[117] This soldier was one of about one hundred deaths in a regiment of nearly a thousand men, and the survivors were weak and weary from months of hard living on the land during their long march from Baton Rouge to Port Hudson. "Our men were walking skeletons," wrote one of them, "ragged, unkempt beyond words."[118] "Comrade Gere," wrote a fellow soldier, "had somewhat anticipated our arrival. His tall, familiar, commanding figure was the first to greet our longing eyes as we pulled up to the Northampton station. He served his country well . . . may his shadow never be less!"[119] Stearns's wife, Sula, along with his brothers and in-laws, doubtless met him at the station in Greenfield, although no one made note of his arrival.

Gere, after all, was a public man, Stearns an obscure figure, and they handled the aftermath of the war just as they had lived before it. Gere never lost his taste for the good fight. In the election of 1872, some abolitionist coadjutants in Northampton (and in other former abolitionist bailiwicks as well), comrades who had stood by him throughout the 1840s and 1850s, threw in the towel and supported the reconciliationist platform of Horace Greeley. Gere excoriated them, snorting that reconciliationism was "the veriest political clap trap." The North had not been harsh or punitive in its treatment of the South, it had been "magnanimous and liberal."[120] Some years later, when his *Hampshire Gazette* reached its centennial, he put out a special edition with the assistance of eighty writers and illustrators who produced scores of short pieces. As the memory of abolitionism faded and a new group of leaders in Northampton did their best to close the book on that chapter, his essay on town politics reminded them of the strength of political abolitionism before the war.[121] In 1902 he published *Reminiscences of Old Northampton: Sketches of the Town as It Appeared from 1840 to 1850,* a fine-grained chronicle of the town's houses, businesses, and personalities that drew heavily on his centennial essays. Its focus on the 1840s was not accidental, for this was the seminal period in Gere's life that marked his abolitionist baptism. He described Northampton as an antislavery "stronghold," and once again recounted the history of the Free Soil and Republican Parties. He also reminded his readers that Northampton was not without sin, for its churches had practiced Jim Crow.[122]

Nor did he repudiate his support for the foreign born. At his death a eulogist wrote that his coverage of immigrants was unerringly "wise and sagacious. He took the ground that foreigners were here to stay, and that they should be recognized in the official distribution of the patronage because such recognition was justly due them and would make them better citizens." Over the fierce objection of the Protestant churches and nativists, he worked in 1892 to elect John O'Donnell, the town's first mayor of Irish extraction.[123]

At age eighty, in 1908, Gere was something of a fascination, one of the oldest working journalists in the area, admired for his pioneering work as a news gatherer. Regional newspapermen feted him at a dinner in nearby Springfield, toasting what a speaker called an "ideal career." When it was his turn to talk, he rose to explain that he attributed his "success" to the "cultivation of . . . local news," the same gift that informed his Civil War reportage.[124] Several years later, just before his death, he betrayed his growing sense of mortality to an interviewer, acknowledging that at this stage in life, "I am looking forward . . . to what there is beyond death. There was a vast amount of bigotry in the old New England stock, but I have lived long enough to see much of it pass away." The vestigial prejudice was regrettable because it reflected "fear," and "fear is the only devil there is." He concluded, "I rest on what I think was the belief of Abraham Lincoln. . . . I now have only a spirit of kindness and charity for all."[125]

No one feted Marshall Stearns in his postwar years. He eventually moved to his family's estate, just beyond the town center, and fathered two more girls with Sula. He followed his brothers into building construction and may well have started a distillery. Sula passed away at age thirty-six, in 1874. Five years later, Stearns again heard the siren call of California, this time to manage a farm or winery. Placing his older daughters in the care of family, he went west by rail with Rosa, his youngest, and stayed there until 1884. He spent his last years in Rosa's care, in another family house in the town center. Family legend has it that toward the end of his years, he could be seen ambling down Main Street on his horse Dandy, on his way to the home of a longtime friend to play checkers.[126]

Stearns's was a retiring and mundane life except in one particular—his relationship with his former assistant at the contraband camp in Baton Rouge. Union officers were either assigned or picked their own servants from the ranks of the camps' fugitives, who worked as butlers, maids, or cooks. Some officers were indifferent to their servants, dryly mentioning them in their correspondence. Gere, for one, told his readers that his staff "had a contraband cook," but did not name him or her.[127] Other Union men expressed appreciation for their help, allowing that it was easy to get used to such an unexpected perk. One Northampton correspondent and captain in the 52nd told his readers that he "secured a colored waiter" within twenty-four hours of landing in Baton

Rouge. His former owner had named him "Doctor," but that caused confusion, because when the captain called for a medic, his servant would show up. So he renamed the man "Essex," after the ironclad ship he had boarded after his flight to freedom. The captain found him "efficient . . . faithful," and so eager for self-improvement that he "taught him a few letters of the alphabet." He also reported that Essex wished to "go north and will go with the Lord's help"—though he apparently did not receive help from the captain.[128] Others joked about taking favored servants back with them. Regimental chaplain John F. Moors, who went through several servants, asked his wife toward the end of his stay if he should bring "our colored boy, Sam Howard, home with me?" He then imagined the easy life: "If I do, keep the garden going; then get into the easiest chair with the newest novel, and call out occasionally, Sam, pick the peas! Sam, dig the potatoes! Sam, put the rooster to bed!"[129]

One writer on the home front imagined a grander scene for African Americans. S. S. Eastman, a sizzling Radical Republican and editor of the *Greenfield Courier,* mused hard and seriously about the condition of freed people in the South during the war. When the veterans of the 52nd settled back into civilian life in the fall of 1863, Eastman's thoughts turned to local grain fields. He dismissed the noxious scenario, promoted by Copperheads and racists, that emancipation would unleash Black hordes on the North, scoffing, "Free them and they'll stay" put. Some might come north, "to seek their fortunes, just as some of our people go south." If Black people did arrive, white people should not fear them, because they needed labor. "The introduction of a few colored laborers in our fields would be a blessing. Thousands of our best workers are gone . . . [and] may never return."[130]

While no one thought that bringing even a "few" Black workers to Connecticut Valley farms was a good idea, remarkably enough, some Union officers in the 52nd did come home with freed people. The much-respected Colonel Halbert Greenleaf left the train with a "negro and his wife," and four other officers "each brought home a likely negro" to Northampton.[131] Their

Greenfield comrades followed suit. Major Henry Winn brought back a "young man of white[r] complexion than any of the regiment, a Louisiana slave." Captain Lucien Stone was said to have returned with a "chattel [as] black as he could be. When asked if he was a runaway, he said he was born and raised in Baltimore, sold into Louisiana, read the President's proclamation a few months ago, staid with his master three days after it went into effect," then fled to the Union army.[132]

It is very difficult to tell what motivated the officers in question. Did Winn intend to put his fair-skinned African American man on display? Did Stone desire cheap labor? Were higher ideals at work? We can assume as much in the case of Winn, because he was a known Radical Republican turned Nationalist in the Gilded Age, but there is no way of knowing for certain.[133] The individuals and families brought home by local soldiers simply disappear from the historical record.

But not, it turns out, in the case of Marshall Stearns. Shortly before he was about to leave Baton Rouge, Maria Kline, a "light-skinned," self-liberated woman who became his assistant at the contraband camp, prevailed on him to take her north. Surprised, even dumbfounded, he explained that it was against protocol to include civilians on military transport—his response clearly a dodge, to judge from the actions of Winn and others. But she had earned his trust, having taught the women in camp to sew and having all but taken over the commissary. He told her that if she still wished to go north once he returned, he would pay to transport both her and her ten-year-old son, Joseph.

The story gets woolier thereafter, because the only source we have is family history, or lore, as it were. The family tale has it that Maria and Joseph came to live with the Stearns family in late 1863 or early 1864, presumably working as a servant and nursemaid for their daughters. After a few years, however, Maria was homesick and tired of the harsh winters, and decided to return home with Joseph. We can probably discount the family's story of how easily she blended into a community that "opened all doors to her." As for Joseph, we are told that he wrote back to Stearns in the summer of 1868 to say that he would like to return north to earn his keep, because wages were much better in Massachusetts than in Louisiana.[134] He worked for the family and at "odd jobs" in town for a few years, then took a position at a factory in nearby Orange. There he was said to have courted a young Black woman who returned his affection, except for his annoying habit of chewing tobacco. He agreed to try a substitute, only to substitute a piece of paper (or rag) soaked with vitriol, and it killed him.[135]

The last we hear of Marshall Stearns comes from a family story about an aging comrade, a soldier who had served with him in Baton Rouge and who attended a dinner at the end of a Memorial Day celebration in 1920 at the Congregational Church, some eighteen years after Stearns's death. On this occasion, Stearns's daughters were told that a grizzled veteran, seated on a bench in the vestry and hunched over his cane, wished to speak with them. The man explained that he'd been wounded at Port Hudson and was taken back to Baton Rouge for medical care, but the hospital was crowded to capacity, so he had to be moved to a deck on one of Farragut's ships. Then Stearns showed up and ordered the soldier moved to his own quarters for medical attention. "I want to shake your hand," he told Katie's sisters, Eunice and Rosa, "your father saved my life . . . he saved my life."[136]

Maybe he did, and maybe he didn't. Uncertainty is the risk we run when we try to shine light on the lives of relatively ordinary figures. Henry Gere, of course, was ordinary only next to the more celebrated men of the era, those who once dominated the historiography of the abolitionist movement and the military history of the Civil War. Gere needed no convincing that slavery was wrong or that the way to right that wrong was to take up arms. His battlefront experience only confirmed his convictions.[137] For his part, Stearns was arguably more typical of Union soldiers, the many who went to war without a fully formed political agenda—least of all abolitionism—beyond their heartfelt attachment to the Union. Most of these soldiers followed Abraham Lincoln's path and, in part because of him, came to emancipationism and in some cases to the higher ground of egalitarianism. Stearns followed the same ground, but at a faster pace. If he didn't advance as far as Gere, he surely became a more decent and enlightened man, someone with a new appreciation of the curse of slavery and with new respect for African Americans. For want of a better term, he became a more complete humanitarian.[138] We can also be certain that this ordinary man, along with his somewhat more celebrated comrade, was partly responsible for the initial photographs of Peter, portraits he originally intended for the intimates in his village. Neither man could have had any idea of the extraordinary fame their images would achieve.

Afterword

As for Peter, his post-emancipation life remains up for debate. The historian David Silkeant, as noted above, has persuasively debunked the *Harper's* story that turned a disheveled and brutalized fugitive from slavery into a heroic Union soldier. Indeed, there's reason to believe he may not have enlisted at all. When Peter arrived at Stearns's contraband camp, he was seen by physicians and army recruiters. Physicians at Baton Rouge and other camps testified that many male fugitives they examined were very badly bruised and scarred. "Not one in fifteen," a recruiter told a leading abolitionist sheet, "is free from the marks of severe lashing. More than one-half are rejected because of disability arising from [the] lashing of whips and the biting of dogs on their calves and thighs."[1] Peter was strong enough to have fled some eighty miles from his plantation in southern Louisiana to Baton Rouge but it's possible that the injuries that disqualified fellow runways from military service also disqualified him. He told his examiners that the beating administered the previous October by his overseer left him "two months in bed sore from the whipping."[2] Even if he healed his wounds and regained his strength, no evidence of service in the Union army has come to light. Of course, Peter may have signed up for one the four Louisiana Native Guard units.[3] A review of the muster rolls of two of them turned up three men named Peter with French surnames (he was a French speaker), any one of whom could have been Peter. But it's impossible to know which one, and besides there is no evidence of their battlefield feats. Peter's military career, if there was one, will likely remain unknown.

We have a better idea of what others made of Peter. The cartes de visite mailed home by soldiers and medics stationed in Louisiana in April and May, followed by stories and package deals of his image in the abolitionist and genteel press in May and June, laid the groundwork for the *Harper's Weekly* story in July that reached many more households. Sales of his photograph were so brisk that in August the *National Anti-Slavery Standard* sold out its copies. By then, Peter was known in the United Kingdom and probably on the Continent as well. The humble enslaved man had become a transatlantic icon thanks to the camera and skillful propagandizing of abolitionists and newly awakened sympathizers.[4]

Recent academic work suggests that the camera recorded several dimensions of the African American experience. Antebellum portraits of prominent Black leaders—Frederick Douglass, Harriet Tubman, Sojourner Truth, and lesser figures—were contrived to project quiet dignity and steely strength. Indeed, some shots of Douglass leave the impression of an arch statesman. Images of ordinary free Black individuals at the time tended to project respectability, as if to underline the promise of freedom and assure fidgety Northerners that emancipation did not equate to social upheaval. In the South early photography often depicted white children in Victorian garb coddled by loyal and loving Black nannies.[5]

The historian Matthew Fox-Amato maintains that Peter's photograph violated such norms because it was edgy, exposing the horrors of slavery rather more graphically than any other medium. Daring as it was to show a nude male body, it was bolder still to show the frightful toll of enslavement—bold enough, it seems, to shock even veteran antislavery crusaders. The image evoked an emotional response that abolitionists exploited during the war to spur on the military effort and afterward to further their claim that Reconstruction didn't go far enough. Raising support, of course, also meant raising money. No image of the time, Fox-Amato plausibly maintains, proved to be such an effective means of prying open pocketbooks. Activists from Garrison to Susan B. Anthony appealed for funds at rallies and demonstrations by flashing images of the now famous fugitive from slavery.[6] Peter struck a mightier blow against slavery as a half-naked civilian than as a soldier in uniform.

My larger point here, however, is not about Peter. Instead, it's about Henry Gere and Marshall Stearns, the two ordinary soldiers whose views of slavery were reinforced in the one case and forged in the other, not from stirring oratory or a provocative image but from what they saw of slavery in the theater of the war. Scholarship on college-educated men who served in the Union army went through the same transformation as Stearns.[7] They entered the war as Unionists but became emancipationists in the course of interacting with African Americans. It was their war within the war—a theme that likely describes the battlefield experience of countless other soldiers as well.

Notes

PREFACE

1. *Hampshire Gazette and Northampton (MA) Courier*, April 6, 1863 (hereafter *HGNC*).

"CHAOTIC FREEDOM" IN CIVIL WAR LOUISIANA

1. Bell Irvin Wiley, *The Life of Billy Yank: The Common Soldier of the Union* (Indianapolis: Bobbs-Merrill, 1951), 40. On the trend toward "comrade over cause," see Gerald F. Linderman, *Embattled Courage: The Experience of Combat in the American Civil War* (New York: Free Press, 1987). See also Reid Mitchell, *The Vacant Chair: The Northern Soldier Leaves Home* (New York: Oxford University Press, 1993).
2. James M. McPherson, *For Cause and Comrades: Why Men Fought in the Civil War* (New York: Oxford University Press, 1997). Also see his *What They Fought For, 1861–1865* (New York: Doubleday, 1994).
3. McPherson, *For Cause and Comrades*, 117–30.
4. Chandra Manning, *What This Cruel War Was Over: Soldiers, Slavery, and the Civil War* (New York: Knopf, 2007), 21. For a similar interpretation, though in

the more limited context of the war in the West, see Mark A. Lause, *Race and Radicalism in the Union Army* (Urbana: University of Illinois Press, 2009). For a comprehensive sampling of the latest literature that ranges from the influence of the home front, popular culture, both secular and religious, and so forth, which I have elided here for the sake of brevity, see Paul A. Cimbala and Randall M. Miller, eds., *Union Soldiers and the Home Front: Wartime Experiences, Postwar Adjustments* (New York: Fordham University Press, 2002).

5. On Stearns, see David A. Cecere, "Carrying the Home Front to War: Soldiers, Race, and New England Culture during the Civil War," in Cimbala and Miller, *Union Soldiers and the Home Front,* 293–323. On Gere's life short of his military service, see Bruce Laurie, *Rebels in Paradise: Sketches of Northampton Abolitionists* (Amherst: University of Massachusetts Press, 2015), 85–115.
6. John Mack Faragher, *A Great and Noble Scheme: The Expulsion of the French Acadians from their American Homeland* (New York: W. W. Norton, 2005).
7. Ira Berlin and Herbert G. Gutman, "Natives and Immigrants, Free Men and Slaves: Urban Immigration in the Antebellum South," *American History Review* 88 (December 1983): 1175–1200, and David T. Gleeson, *The Irish in the South, 1815–1877* (Chapel Hill: University of North Carolina Press, 2001).
8. Ira Berlin, *Generations of Captivity: A History of Afri-*

can American Slaves (Cambridge, MA: Harvard University Press, 2003), table 3.

9. John W. Blassingame, *Black New Orleans* (Chicago: University of Chicago Press, 1973), 1–24 and 173–210; and David C. Rankin, "The Politics of Caste: Free Colored Leadership in New Orleans during the Civil War," in *Louisiana's Black Heritage*, ed. Robert R. MacDonald et al. (New Orleans: Louisiana State Museum, 1979), 107–46. Also Laura Foner, "The Free Colored People in Louisiana and St. Domingue: A Comparative Portrait of Two Three-Caste Societies," *Journal of Social History* 3 (Summer 1970): 406–30.

10. Richard Follett, *The Sugar Masters: Planters and Slaves in Louisiana's Cane World, 1820–1860* (Baton Rouge: Louisiana State University Press, 2005), 21. Also Joseph Karl Menn, *The Large Slaveholders of Louisiana—1860* (New Orleans: Pelican, 1964); John Alfred Heitmann, *The Modernization of the Louisiana Sugar Industry, 1830–1910* (Baton Rouge: Louisiana State University Press, 1987); and John C. Rodrigue, *Reconstruction in the Cane Fields: From Slavery to Free Labor in Louisiana's Sugar Parishes, 1862–1880* (Baton Rouge: Louisiana State University Press, 2001). For a long view of graphic representations of the industrial quality of sugar plantations, see John E. Crowley, "Sugar Machines: Picturing Industrialized Slavery," *American Historical Review* 121 (April 2016): 403–36.

11. Eugene Genovese, *The World the Slaveholders Made: Two Essays in Interpretation* (New York: Pantheon, 1969); as well as Roll, Jordan, *Roll: The World the Slaves Made* (New York: Pantheon, 1974). The first of many refutations of this work is James Oakes, *The Ruling Race: A History of American Slaveholders* (New York: Vintage, 1982). Also see James Oakes, *Slavery and Freedom: An Interpretation of the Old South* (New York: Knopf, 1990); and *Edward Baptist, The Half Has Never Been Told: Slavery and the Making of American Capitalism* (New York: Basic Books, 2014).
12. James L. Huston, *Calculating the Value of the Union: Slavery, Property Rights, and the Economic Origins of the Civil War* (Chapel Hill: University of North Carolina Press, 2003).
13. Follett, *Sugar Masters,* 151–66.
14. *Born in Slavery: Slave Narratives from the Federal Writers' Project, 1936–1938,* Library of Congress, vol. 16, parts 1–4, 1:76 (hereafter *BIS*). I have used the online edition of this collection.
15. Ibid., 63.
16. Ibid., 118.
17. Ibid., 202–3, 205–6, and 211–12. For a comparative perspective, see Peter Kolchin, "Reevaluating the American Slave Community: A Comparative Perspective," *Journal of American History* 70 (1983): 579–601, and Richard Dunn, *A Tale of Two Plantations: Life and Labor in Jamaica and Virginia* (Cambridge, MA: Harvard University Press, 2014).

18. *BIS*, 3, 41.

19. Solomon Northup, *Twelve Years a Slave: A Citizen of New York, Kidnapped in Washington City in 1841, and Rescued in 1853 from a Cotton Plantation Near the Red River, in Louisiana*, ed. Sue Eakin and Joseph Logsdon (1853; repr., Baton Rouge: Louisiana State University Press, 1968), 181–83, quote on 183. Also see Adam Rothman, "The Horrors *12 Years a Slave* Couldn't Tell: What a Civil War Soldier's Diary Tells Us about Solomon Northup's Ordeal," *AlJazeera America*, January 18, 2014, http://america.aljazeera.com/opinions/2014/1/the-horrors-a-12years aslaveacouldnattello.html. See also Herbert G. Gutman, *Slavery and the Numbers Game: A Critique of Time on the Cross* (Urbana: University of Illinois Press, 1975), especially 28–29.

20. *BIS* 3:69. See also 4:131–32.

21. Follett, *Slave Masters*, 67–78, quote on 67.

22. *BIS* 4:189.

23. Quoted in Follett, *Sugar Masters*, 67.

24. John D. Winters, *The Civil War in Louisiana* (Baton Rouge: Louisiana State University Press, 1963), 8–10. Also Robert W. Shugg, *Origins of the Class War in Louisiana* (Baton Rouge: Louisiana State University Press, 1939), 157–70; Charles P. Dew, "Who Won the Secession Election in Louisiana?," *Journal of Southern History* 36 (February, 1970): 18–32; and Donald E. Reynolds, *Texas Terror: The Slave Insurrection Panic of 1860 and the Secession of the Lower South*

(Baton Rouge: Louisiana State University Press, 2007).

25. For instance, Brig. Gen. [F. or T.?] Williams to Major G. C. Strong, Baton Rouge, June 6, 1862, and William Kilbourn to Gen. Benjamin Butler, Baton Rouge, June 20, 1862, part 1, box 1, Records of the US Army Continental Commands, 1861–1920, Dept. of the Gulf, Letters Received, National Archives, Washington, DC (hereafter ACC).

26. Winters, *Civil War in Louisiana,* 9–205. Also James M. McPherson, *Battle Cry of Freedom: The Civil War Era* (New York: Oxford University Press, 1988), 626–65, and Bruce Levine, *The Fall of the House of Dixie: The Civil War and the Social Revolution that Transformed the South* (New York: Random House, 2013), 107–70.

27. Winters, *Civil War in Louisiana,* 9–10, 111–23, and 166–67.

28. Levine, *Fall of the House of Dixie,* 115, 118, and 122. Also see John Syrett, "The Confiscation Acts: The North Strikes Back," in Cimbala and Miller, *Uncommon Time,* 280–326.

29. C. Peter Ripley, *Slaves and Freedmen in Civil Slaves and Freedmen in Civil War Louisiana,* (Baton Rouge: Louisiana State University Press, 1976): 25–101; and Eric Foner, *Reconstruction: America's Unfinished Revolution, 1863–1877* (New York: Harper & Row, 1988), 35–76. For a particularly vivid picture of the disorder in Louisiana in the spring of 1863, see

Louis S. Gerteis, *From Contraband to Freedman: Federal Policy toward Southern Blacks, 1861–1865* (Westport, CT: Greenwood Press, 1973).

30. John S. Clark, Capt., Vt., 18th Vols., to Col. R. B. Irwin, January 30, 1863, Box 2, 1862–1865, ACC.

31. Col. C. C. Auger, Maj. Gen. [unnamed unit], April 8, 1863, to Col. R. B. Irwin, Box 2, 1862–1865, ACC.

32. For instance, J. Fas and [illeg.] to N. P. Banks, January 2, 1863, ACC.

33. J[ohn] F. Moors, *History of the Fifty-Second Regiment Massachusetts Volunteers by the Chaplain* (Boston: George H. Ellis, 1893), 158. See also Ripley, *Slaves and Freedmen in Civil War Louisiana,* 98–101. Capt. T. N. Austin of the Massachusetts 52nd told his diary that "ten of the leaders" were lynched; Ripley put the number at four. See also Capt. L. H. Stone to Provost Marshal A. B. Long, April 25, 1863, and Col. S. G. Jerrad to Asst. Adjutant General R. B. Irwin, April 28, 1863, as cited in Gerteis, *From Contraband to Freedman,* 219n55. It appears that the Black "insurrectionist[s]," a group of "straggling soldiers" from African American regiments, were led by a Creole named Theodule Melancon. He was jailed by a contingent of the Massachusetts 52nd, but his fate and additional details of the gruesome episode are unknown. I was unable to find press coverage.

34. *L'Union / The Union* (New Orleans), July 14, 1863.

35. *Hampshire Gazette and Northampton (MA) Courier,* June 9, 1863.

36. *Northampton Courier,* April 17, 1855.
37. Laurie, *Rebels in Paradise,* 85–115.
38. *HGNC,* August 26 and September 16, 1862.
39. Ethel F. Jackson, "What the Stearns Family Was Like" (unpublished manuscript, undated), Marshall Spring Stearns and Stearns Family Papers, 1862–1863, Special Collections, State Library of Massachusetts, State House, Boston (hereafter SFP). Quote on 32. This manuscript is also held at the Northfield (Massachusetts) Historical Society (hereafter NHS).
40. Ibid.
41. Marshall S. Stearns to Sula H. Stearns, December 2, 1862, SFP.
42. MSS to SHS, December 12, 1862, SFP.
43. MSS to SHS, March 25, 1863, SFP.
44. MSS to SHS, April 19, 1863, SFP.
45. MSS to SHS, April 28, 1863, SFP.
46. MSS to SHS, March 23, 1863, SFP.
47. MSS to SHS, March 25, 1863, SFP.
48. MSS to SHS, April 14, 1863, SFP.
49. MSS to SHS, April 16 and 19, 1863, SFP.
50. American Antislavery Society, *Fifth Annual Report* (New York: American Antislavery Society, 1838), 135.
51. Moors, *History of the Fifty-Second;* see muster lists at the end of the text, n.p.
52. James K. Hosmer, *The Color-Guard: Being a Corporal's Notes of Military Service in the Nineteenth Army*

Corps (Boston: Walker, Wise, and Company, 1864), 9 and 31.

53. Ibid., 9.

54. For instance, MSS to Best Friend, April 14, 1863, SFP.

55. MSS to SHS, December 14, 1862, SFP.

56. MSS to SHS, January 21, 1863, SFP.

57. Ibid.

58. MSS to Mother, March 11, 1863, SFP.

59. MSS to SHS, December 23, 1862, and April 12, 1863, SFP. About 2,000 were in his camp and another 2,500 or so on the nearby government plantations he was charged with managing.

60. Ethel F. Jackson, "Three Centuries of the Stearns Family, 1600–1900" (unpublished manuscript, 1939), 20, SFP. A copy of this typescript is also at the NHS.

61. Ibid. Also MSS to SHS, May 30, 1863, SFP. While this is not the place to delve into the historiography of the contraband camps, it must be noted that conditions ranged from barely tolerable to lethal. Even the handful of the well-provisioned and orderly camps in the Upper South became overwhelmed by escaped enslaved people as the war wore on. Camps throughout Dixie were burdened by inadequate supplies and insufficient medical care; even worse were the heat, poor sanitation, and overcrowding that led to disease and horrific death rates.

It is, to say the least, interesting that in their letters neither Stearns nor Gere mentioned these terrible conditions. Their silence remains a mystery. The most comprehensive (and dark) account of the camps is from Jim Downs, *Sick from Freedom: African-American Illness and Suffering during the Civil War* (New York: Oxford University Press, 2012). See also Cam Walker, "Corinth: The Story of a Contraband Camp," *Civil War History* 20 (March 1974): 5–22; Noralee Frankel, *Freedom's Women: Black Women and Families in Civil War Mississippi* (Bloomington: Indiana University Press, 1999), especially 35–39; and Steven V. Ash, *The Black Experience in the Civil War* (New York: Praeger, 2010), 42–43 and 63–64. For valuable contemporaneous accounts by women who worked as teachers and caregivers in schools and the camps, see Henry L. Swift, ed., *Dear Ones at Home: Letters from Contraband Camps* (Nashville, TN: Vanderbilt University Press, 1966); and Laura S. Haviland, *A Woman's Life-Work: Labors and Experiences* (Chicago: C. V. Waite & Company, 1887).

62. MSS to SHS, January 4, 1863, SFP.
63. MSS to SHS, December 23, 1862, SFP.
64. Cecere, "Carrying the Home Front to War," 320.
65. Moors, *History of the Fifty-Second,* 101–3, quote on 102.
66. Ibid., 130–32, quote on 131.
67. Ira Berlin et al., eds., *Freedom: A Documentary History of Emancipation, 1861–1867,* ser. 1, vol. 1 (New

York: Cambridge University Press, 1985), 244–45. For more on Long, see Moors, *History of the Fifty-Second,* lvi–lvii.

68. MSS to Mother, January 8, 1863, in Jackson, "Stearns Family," 62.
69. Moors, *History of the Fifty-Second,* 215.
70. *HGNC,* February 14, 1863.
71. *HGNC,* January 6, 1863.
72. Ibid.
73. Ibid.
74. Ibid.
75. *HGNC,* February 3, 1863.
76. *HGNC,* February 24, 1863.
77. Ibid.
78. *HGNC,* May 5, 1863.
79. *HGNC,* March 10, 1863.
80. *HGNC,* March 17,1863.
81. *HGNC,* February 10, 1863.
82. *HGNC,* March 24, 1863.
83. *HGNC,* June 9, 1863.
84. *HGNC,* March 17, 1863.
85. *HGNC,*, June 9, 1863.
86. *HGNC,* January 1 and January 20, 1863.
87. *HGNC,* July 14, 1863.
88. *Harper's Weekly,* July 4, 1863.
89. Ibid.
90. *Liberator*, June 12, 1863.
91. For instance, Margaret Abruzzo, *Polemical Pain: Slavery, Cruelty, and the Rise of Humanitarianism*

(Baltimore: Johns Hopkins University Press, 2011), 201–3; and Carol Emberton, *Beyond Redemption: Race, Violence, and the American South after the Civil War* (Chicago: University of Chicago Press, 2013), 102–3.

92. Emberton, *Beyond Redemption*, 103.

93. See his wartime images at Historic Northampton, Northampton, MA. This striking carte de visite is found in other repositories as well. For instance, an identical version entitled "Contraband Yard," by J. W. Taft, is in series 1, Visual Material, box 11, folder 498, by J. W. Taft, Oak Gallery, Memphis, TN, in the Randolph Linsy Simpson African-American Collection, Yale Collection of American Literature, Beinecke Rare Book and Manuscript Library, Yale University, New Haven, CT. Taft may have made his own copy from the original negative, but there is no doubt that the original image was by McPherson and Oliver. The one printed in figure 6 is in the G. H. Suydam Collection (Mss. 1394), item #1394009r, Louisiana and Lower Mississippi Collections, Louisiana State University Libraries, Baton Rouge.

94. See, for instance, Andrea Volpe, "The Cartes-de-Visite Craze," *The Onion Pages*, August 6, 2013, and Andrea Volpe, "Cartes-de-Visite Portrait Photographs and the Culture of Class Formation," in *The Middling Sorts: Explorations in the History of the Middle Classes*, ed. Barton J. Bledstein and Robert D. Johnston (New York: Routledge, 2001), 157–69.

95. David Silkenat, "A Typical Negro: Gordon, Peter, and Vincent Colyer, and the Story behind Slavery's Most Famous Photograph," *American Nineteenth Century History* 15 (August 2014): 169–86, quote on 169.
96. Ibid., 174.
97. Cassandra Jackson, *Violence, Visual Culture, and the Black Male Body* (New York: Routledge, 2011), 28.
98. Ibid., 171–73. The different appearance of Peter's and Gordon's hair is in dispute. In *Polemical Pain,* Margaret Abruzzo identifies Peter as "a shaved Gordon," which could imply that Gordon was photographed first (202–3). With better evidence, David Silkenat maintains that Peter was photographed first, which suggests that his hair had grown back in by the end of April. This seems more plausible, if we assume that Stearns had Peter cleaned up and shaved before he took him to the photographer.
99. *New York Tribune,* December 3, 1863. Also Silkenat, "Typical Negro," 180–82.
100. Ibid.
101. "Scourged Back" (unpublished manuscript), National Archives, Washington, DC. I used the online version.
102. These are filed in Gere's Civil War photographs, Historic Northampton, Northampton, MA.
103. *HGNC,* April 6, 1863.

104. MSS to SHS, April 12, 1863, SFP.
105 MSS to Best Friend, April 14, 1863, SFP.
106 www.Escaped-Slave-Gordon-CDV-Portrait-1863.png. MSS The interesting feature of this image, apart from the production date printed between the portrait and the handwritten text, is that it was one of at least two taken in early April, not the one taken at the end of April that became so famous. It suggests that pictures of Peter were circulating a month before the iconic one was made and three months before the *Harper's* story appeared. Why assistant surgeon Mercer felt compelled to send it at this time is not known. He left no papers.
107. *HGNC,* April 6, 1863. On the Bridgemans, see *Hampshire County Journal* (Northampton, MA), October 1887, and *American Stationer* (NY), May 17, 1894.
108. *HGNC,* May 5, 1863.
109. Quotes in Silkenat, "Typical Negro," 173. Original in *Independent* (NY), May 28, 1863.
110. Silkenat, "Typical Negro," 173–76.
111. *Liberator,* June 12, 1863.
112. Ibid., 54.
113. See Silkenat, "Typical Negro," 173. Also Kathleen Collins, "The Scourged Back," *History of Photography* 9 (January–March 1985): 43–45.
114. Peter Palmquist and Thomas R. Kailbourn, *Pioneer Photographers from the Mississippi to the Conti-*

nental Divide (Stanford, CA: Stanford University Press, 2005), 430–31.

115. See https://louisianadigitallibrary.org/islandora/search/mods_subject_topic_ms%3A%22McPherson%2C%5C%20William%5C%20D.%2C%5C%20photographer%22 for his surviving portfolio.

116. Ibid., numbers 101, 102, 151, and 116.

117. *Greenfield (MA) Courier,* August 10, 1863 (hereafter *GC*).

118. Moors, *History of the Fifty-Second,* 214. Also see *HGNC,* August 4, 1863.

119. Moors, *History of the Fifty-Second,* 215.

120. *HGNC,* October 1, 1872.

121. *HGNC,* September 6 and 20, 1886. These pieces were published together in the commemorative volume *Centennial Hampshire Gazette* (Northampton, MA: Hampshire Gazette, 1886), Mortimer Rare Book Room, Smith College, Northampton, MA.

122. Henry S. Gere, *Reminiscences of Old Northampton: Sketches of the Town as It Appeared from 1840 to 1850* (Northampton, MA: Gazette Printing Company, 1902), 132.

123. *Daily Hampshire Gazette* (Northampton, MA), March 26, 1914 (hereafter *DHG*).

124. *DHG,* May 1, 1908.

125. *DHG,* March 27, 1914.

126. Jackson, "Three Centuries of the Stearns Family."

127. *HGNC,* January 6, 1863.
128. *HGNC,* February 17, 1863.
129. Moors, *History of the Fifty-Second,* 62 and 148.
130. *GC,* November 24 and December 1,1863.
131. *HGNC,* August 11, 1863.
132. *GC,* August 10, 1863.
133. On Winn, see Henry F. Bedford, *Socialism and the Workers in Massachusetts, 1886–1912* (Amherst: University of Massachusetts Press, 1966), 18–19. Also *Springfield (MA) Republican,* October 17, 1900, and *Boston Herald,* June 27, 1908. Winn, the only member of the 52nd to hail from Boston, may well have been "Bostonian," who penned the letter in December 1863 that clarified the identities of Peter and Gordon.
134. Jackson, " Stearns Family," 72, cites Joseph's letter to Marshall dated July 7, 1868, but the original letter has disappeared.
135. Ibid., 72–73.
136. Ibid., 74.
137. Gere, of course, was a politico. For an example of a common soldier in the 52nd who saw the war through the eyes of a devout Christian and who sympathized with African Americans from this point of view, see the letters signed "L" in *HGNC* from December 1862 to June 1863. The writer, Daniel W. Lyman of Easthampton, was one of the youngest members of the regiment and the only soldier to be killed in battle at the siege of Port

Hudson in June 1863. See Moors, *History of the Fifty-Second,* lxii–lxiii. For a soldier who evolved only so far on the question of equality, see David W. Blight, ed., *When This Cruel War Is Over: The Civil War Letters of Charles Harvey Brewster* (Amherst: University of Massachusetts Press, 1992).

138. For an interpretation of him as a "paternalist," with all that implies, see Cecere, "Carrying the Home Front to War." It is interesting to note that other soldiers developed along a similar trajectory as Stearns, most notably Henry T. Johns, a private in the 49th Massachusetts, who, it should be said, was rather more of a Christian than Stearns, but quite as liberal-minded as Lyman. The Deerfield minister, who was awarded the Medal of Honor for valor at Port Hudson, sprinkled the early months of his memoir with aspersions on "anti-slavery men" and doubts about the mental capacity of African Americans. However, the more he saw of slavery up close and heard from runaways, the more space he devoted to them and with growing disgust for Southerners and respect for African Americans. By the end of his service he wrote in the wake of the New York Draft Riots, "All honor to negro soldiers. They deserve citizenship. They will secure it." See Henry T. Johns, *Life with the 49th Massachusetts Volunteers* (Washington, DC: Ramsey and Bisbee, 1890), quotes on 141 and 386–87.

Laura S. Haviland, the intrepid Quaker abolitionist who worked as a teacher in the Mississippi Valley through the war and Reconstruction, offered a similar observation on the impact of slavery on soldiers. She not only wrote movingly of the Black women at a camp in Cairo, Illinois, who arrived dressed in rags, malnourished, and pining for husbands and children sold away from them; she also observed, "Such are some of the incidents that gradually changed the politics of the army. They made our Butlers and Hunters by scores. They saw that man's inhumanity to man was the outgrowth of slavery. They clearly perceived that the iron rod of oppression must be broken, or the unholy rebellion would succeed." Haviland, *Woman's Life-Work,* 255. Haviland clearly exaggerated here. For every soldier who was transformed by the impact of slavery on the Black population, many more doubtless remained unmoved; such soldiers saw the wretchedness, illiteracy, and expressive religiosity of fugitives as evidence of their barbarity. I am not arguing here for something so patently silly as a wholesale turn against slavery, only that firsthand experiences with escaped enslaved people and slavery transformed some soldiers into emancipationists, or reinforced their abolitionist convictions. I am also suggesting that historians have not fully appreciated this aspect of the conflict.

AFTERWORD

1. "The Cruelties of Slavery," *National Anti-Slavery Standard,* July 4, 1863.
2. *Photograph of Peter, an Enslaved Man Who Was Whipped by an Overseer,* Photographs from the Joseph H. Taylor Album, ca. 1861–ca. 1865, Records of the War Department General and Special Staffs, 1860–1952, National Archives, Washington, DC, https://catalog.archives.gov/id/533232.
3. James G. Hollandsworth Jr., Louisiana *Native Guards: The Black Military Experience during the Civil War* (Baton Rouge: Lousiana State University Press, 1998).
4. David Silkenat, "A Typical Negro: Gordon, Peter, and Vincent Colyer, and the Story behind Slavery's Most Famous Photograph," *American Nineteenth Century History* 15 (August 2014): 173–76; and *Matthew Fox-Amato, Exposing Slavery: Photography, Human Bondage, and the Birth of Modern Visual Politics* (New York: Oxford University Press, 2019), 171–81.
5. Deborah Willis and Barbara Krauthamer, *Envisioning Emancipation: Black Americans and the End of Slavery* (Philadelphia: Temple University Press, 2013), 3–37. Of course there were also the portraits of African-born enslaved men and women commissioned by the Harvard anthropologist Lewis Agassiz to "prove" his theory of polygenesis—separate origins of the white and Black races (4–7).

6. Fox-Amato, *Exposing Slavery,* 174–81.
7. Bruce Laurie, "'Some of the Sweetest Christians': The Wartime Education of Amherst's Boys in Blue," in *Amherst in the World,* ed. Martha Saxton (Amherst, MA: Amherst College Press, 2020): 305–24.